HOW TO TAKE YOUR BUSINESS TO NEW HEIGHTS

JEN DU PLESSIS

America's Mortgage Mentor

FOREWORD BY **MICHAEL J. MAHER**, *THE SEVEN LEVELS OF COMMUNICATION*

Quantity sales special discounts are available on quantity purchases by corporations, associations, and others. For details, contact the publisher at the address above.

Orders by U.S. trade bookstores and wholesalers. Email info@ BeyondPublishing.net

The Beyond Publishing Speakers Bureau can bring authors to your live event. For more information or to book an event contact the Beyond Publishing Speakers Bureau speak@BeyondPublishing.net

The Author can be reached directly at JenDuPlessis.com

Manufactured and printed in the United States of America distributed globally by BeyondPublishing.net

BEYOND
PUBLISHING

New York | Los Angeles | London | Sydney

ISBN Softcover: 978-1-949873-51-1

ISBN Hardcover: 978-1-637920-62-6

Brian Du Plessis - from Sandy to Danny. Thank you for being my rock and supporting me unconditionally. I'm sure there is more to say about one's husband but for me, you have always allowed my career to be the front runner. I feel it takes a strong man to be behind a woman, but even a stronger man to take stand behind an even stronger woman! Thank you for always working on "the Jen Project," carrying my bags, running security, and driving the car!

Dave H. Stevens - my manager over 20 years ago. You had such an impact on my career. You are such a positive personality, a forward thinker, and a great presenter. I learned most of what I know from you. You have always been the one who would hear me out when I was making major decisions, who supported me, who laughed with me about the crazy things we did way back when we were in business, both in our late 20s and early 30s.

"I wish I had read this book 20 years ago! People start businesses with high hopes but lack the skills and the plan necessary to make it successful-this book eliminates that problem. It is an easy read with step-by-step instructions from a real pro. So stop repeating what doesn't work or floundering around for a solution. Read LAUNCH! and make success happen."

- Joan Coullahan, CFDS

"If this book doesn't motivate you to succeed, NOTHING WILL! *LAUNCH!* is today's GPS for how to build, grow and thrive in your business. Tailored to the mortgage industry, its principles, step-by-step instructions, and honest straight-talk are applicable to any business. The You of yesterday will stop talking and take action! Jen Du Plessis tells and shows us how to get it done...NOW!"

Carla Williams, Realtor, RE/MAX Premier

"Jen is a great leader and educator in the mortgage industry. She is not only respected as a top producer but for the teaching she does to both consumers and real estate professionals. Her advice is always of high value, and I think that this book would benefit anyone wanting to understand how real estate finances work."

- Barry Habib, CEO of MBS Highway

"The core of this book is truly caring for other people and their success. Jennifer has a way of transferring her passion to others in a special way that encourages them to take action. It is another way she is leaving a legacy for the benefit of others."

Gerald P. Rothm an, Jr., Mortgage Broker

"In a world where loan officers are constantly in fear of being replaced by robots, regulators are slashing paychecks, and the man hours it takes to produce a loan are roughly triple that of 15 years ago, today's originators need to read AND APPLY the lessons found in this book! Coach Jen does a masterful job sharing simple, easy-to-implement strategies guaranteed to ignite your growth.

If you have ever met Jen, you know that she is an amazingly energetic and enthusiastic speaker and coach. And her boundless energy and passion can definitely be felt in the message of these pages. You'll walk away from this book with a renewed sense of purpose and an explosive amount of excitement and encouragement to propel your- self to the next level. And if you actually APPLY the strategies outlined here, the sky's the limit to your growth potential!"

- Erik Janeczko, Maximum Acceleration Head Coach

"I have known and worked with Jennifer for several decades and expe rienced her amazing success and her ability to communicate and lead others on their respective paths to success as well. Jennifer is unique in her ability to clearly understand and articulate the pathway to be a top performer, and she has spent years crafting this skill in a way that results in proven success for herself and others. Jennifer is self-driven, has an amazing enthusiasm for ever improving on her performance and success, and is infectious with her attitude. I highly recommend that others read, learn, and practice her skills. Proven success pat terns cannot be denied, and she has a clear history of success."

- David H Stevens, President and CEO Mo rtgag e Bankers Association

"Jen helped me create and put into practice a living business plan, introduced me to influencers that have changed the way I do business, and so much more. Jen did all of this without expectation of reciproca tion. She has a giver's heart and recognizes the value in mentoring and loving others. I appreciate her candor, and I am thankful that she's so willing to give her input."

- Katrina M. Smith, Realtor

"This is a must read for all sales professionals."

- Tony Thompson, CMB, Founder /CEO NAM MBA

"Jen is the absolute best! She has simplified my business plan, taught me that I need to slow down to speed up, and now I am engaged with top realtors and referral partners. Since I have been working with Jen, my business has increased, my relationships have gone deeper, I work less, and I have more clarity in what I am doing. She cares, she is bril liant, she is completely 100% awesome! Her book is spot on and easy to apply."

- Paul Olbrantz, Loan Adviser

LAUNCH!

HOW TO TAKE YOUR BUSINESS TO NEW HEIGHTS

JEN DU PLESSIS

America's Mortgage Mentor

FOREWORD BY **MICHAEL J. MAHER**, *THE SEVEN LEVELS OF COMMUNICATION*

By Michael J. Maher

You are a Catalyst. You are special. You are making a difference. You are making an impact. You get a chance and a choice every day to be a negative or positive influence on those around you.

Chumps, Chimps, and Champs. I've told my son that in every situation he can choose to be one of three people: He can be a Chump, a Chimp, or a Champ. Chumps are negative leaders. People who seek trouble and seek to have oth ers get in trouble with them. Rather than choosing the right thing to do, they choose to be a nuisance, be a naysayer or break the rules, perhaps even break the law. They convince others to follow along in the spirit of "let's have some fun" or "lighten up" or "they deserve it." Those who follow are the Chimps.

The Chimps merely follow. They mimic the leaders' words, behaviors, and actions. In many cases, without thinking about it. In a desperate need to fit in or wanting to be part of a group, any group, the Chimps are not old enough, mature enough, or strong enough to lead, so they must follow. If you are going to be a Chimp, which we all need to do at some point in our lives, we need to follow positive leaders. These are the Champs.

Champs are positive leaders. They choose to help, to serve, to do good, and to do well. When others are choosing to go down the path of drugs, alcohol, or even just making fun of another, the Champ chooses the right path. Walks away, brings others, and chooses to do the right thing.

In some cases, my son has been the Chump. In others, the Chimp. Luckily, as he learns, grows, and matures, he is choosing the way of the Champ more often than the others.

Be a Champ. Learn from Champs. Jennifer Du Plessis could have very easily gone down the path of the Chump. I can't wait for you to read her story. All the limiting beliefs you may harbor will be released! In the absence of a lot of positive mentors, many choose the path of being Chimps following Chumps. It's the easy thing to do. Poverty, alcoholism, gender... all are ready excuses for going down the path of the Chump or Chimp. But instead Jennifer chose to be a Champ. And like all Champs, she is willing to share her wisdom.

It's a SYSTEM. Jennifer leads you down a path of excellence. From your manage ment of time and energy to exactly what to do to produce amazing numbers in sales, she explains every step in vivid detail while also relating stories from her career as one of the top producing sales people in the history of mortgages. I've always said SYSTEM is an acronym for Saving You Stress, Time, Energy, and Money, and within these pages, Jennifer gives you strategies, systems, and pro cesses to save you stress, time, energy, and money. You'll love her segments on Learning, Earning, and Returning and defining your role as a Finder, Minder, or Grinder. You will repeatedly refer to this book as a resource.

Written To Help People. Accomplishing the monumental task of writing and finish ing a book is something to admire. Those who make it happen dedicate countless hours writing, editing, thinking, re-thinking through the readers' minds, and plan ning the layout of the book. It is like raising a child from birth through their teen age years-trust me, there are tears, yelling, and frustration with the book-writing process. When it is finished, it is much like sending your only child to college. You've done all you can. Now your "child" is off to the "real world"-a world full of Chumps and Chimps. Something you've poured your heart and soul into is now open to feedback, criticism, and 1-star reviews. As authors, we need to remember that the book was not written to please people. It was written to help people. Jennifer Du Plessis has given you the road map and the blueprint to better your business. She has given you the plan and the program to be a Champ-The Path of Champions. Are you ready to take the first step?

Michael J. Maher is the best-selling author of *(II) The Seven levels of Communication: Go from Relationships to Referrals and co-author of The Miracle Morning for Real Estate Agents.* The CEO of REFERCO, the World's Foremost Authority on Business Referrals, Michael is also known as *North America's Most Referred Real Estate Professional.* He is the proud father and founder of the *Generosity Generation.* You can learn more at REFERCO.com or TheBookOnReferrals.com.

Table of Contents

SECTION 5. MINDER

SECTION 6. GRINDER

SECTION 7. WHAT HAPPENS NEXT?

SECTION 1.
INTRODUCTION

✳ Why This Book?

> **The Big Idea:** This book offers tools, advice, strategies, and inspiration from my experience to help you spark growth in your mortgage practice.
>
> *"DO the stuff to get the results!"*
>
> *- Jen Du Plessis*

I want you to be fabulously successful in the mortgage lending industry. No, scratch that! I want you to be successful beyond your wildest dreams, whether in business or your personal life, using mortgage lending as the stepping stone to get there.

Believe me when I say that tremendous success is possible. You can do it! This book is about tools, advice, strategies, and especially inspiration to spark growth in your practice. It's my hope that each and every one of you use what you read in this book to boost your practice to new heights.

I'm so excited to help you achieve your dreams. I wish I could talk one-on-one with you so you could feel the excitement in my voice and see the excitement in my eyes when I talk about how to ignite your practice. But since I'll probably never get around to personally visiting every one of you, I hope you will feel my excitement through these printed words.

I've been teaching, training, coaching, and speaking for many years. Sharing and helping people reach for their dreams is a driving force in my life. But something that has been missing is sharing my experiences on a broader scale. My greatest hope for this book is to get my message out to you so you believe in yourself.

I really want to see people stay in this business for a long, long time. I've seen scores of people come and go. What I want for you is a career in this business, not just a job. It's the difference between being in the business for one year at a time for 30 years, and being in the business for 30 years and seeing your business grow and grow every year. That's the place I hope I can help you get to.

The experiences and ideas I share in this book are for you if you're just getting into the business. This book is also for you if you're struggling and need some help and tips to get you over that hump. And this book is also for you if you're a seasoned professional just like me and you want some golden nuggets or extra ideas to keep your momentum going. believe you should try to learn from anyone who can help your mortgage practice grow. Learn from loan officers who are doing millions and millions in loans every month, year after year. Learn from loan officers who are new in the business and can bring some fresh ideas to us veterans. Learn from real estate agents, title companies, and other referral partners, such as financial planners and attorneys. Work to understand their perspectives, because these partners play such a huge role in your success as an originator.

What I want you to know is that I'm just an ordinary person. I'm grateful that I've been able to do some extraordinary things in my career in this business, and I know you can, too. Allow me to share my experience and knowledge to spark or re-spark your practice. We're about to fuel things up with an intensity like you've never seen. You're going to reach heights that you haven't imagined before now.

And if not now, when? As you read this book, act on the ideas right away. If you're reading in the evening at home, write down something that you'll act on the next day. If you're reading on the weekend, write down five ideas that you will act on-one day after the other-for the next five days. Stop waiting and talking about your future success. The time is now!

I want to shock you into action. If you're not moving forward in this business, you're moving backward, because things change so much and so constantly. You can't stand still. So take the ideas you'll find in these pages, act on them right away, and work on them consistently day after day. You'll see a huge difference in your practice and your life.

And I absolutely want to hear about your successes! When you use a nugget or an idea from this book and it helps create a spark in your practice, tell me about it! Tell me what you did, tell me how you applied the idea to your life and your practice, and tell me how it worked. Email me at

success@kineticsparkconsulting.com.

Let's get started, shall we?

✳ Returning What I've Learned

> **The Big Idea:** Awaken the spark that is within you so you can make your life grand
>
> "We all have two choices:
> We can make a living or we can design a life."
>
> -Jim Rohn

To start us off, I feel the need to tell you more about my why...

I've come to believe that our lives are marked by three stages. First we learn, then we earn, and then we return. For the first 20 or so years we learn-we mold ourselves into who we will become. Then we take that knowledge and who we are out into the real world, and we earn and produce for 20, 30, 40, or more years. We climb the proverbial ladder of success. At some point during the mature stage of that earning period, we realize it's time to return, time for us to pass on our experience to others so they can grow and improve on what we've accomplished.

I've always lived by the premise that every day I can-and should-help or change someone else's life, even if by the smallest of gestures. So, it's natural for me to want to return what I've learned and experienced in the mortgage lending industry.

What I hope to do is inspire each and every one of you reading this book to excel in this industry so you can live a life of quality for many decades. As you pursue happiness, I want you to be happy along the way. And I want to help you reach new heights, heights that you previously never even imagined you would reach.

Now, you might not believe you can reach those heights right now, but I'm absolutely certain you can. Why am I so confident? Because I've done it. If anyone ever had the deck stacked against them early in life, it was me! I know if I can reach remarkable success, you can be even more remarkable!

"Jenny Who Ain't Got a Penny"

When I was a child, my destiny was most certainly not pointed toward success. A rocky, lonely childhood would be an understated way of describing where I started from. I was an only child until I was 13, with parents who fought nearly every day of my childhood. My father was an alcoholic who surrendered his life to the bottle, and my parents' marriage was dysfunctional at boot.

Many a time, my mother forced me to go into a bar to tell my father that it was time to come home, threatening to leave me at the bar if I couldn't convince him. Dad would disappear for weeks at a time while on a drinking binge. And on many occasions, I saw my father holding a shotgun to my mother's head. My mother and father worked all the time, but we were still poor and isolated.

In contrast, my five uncles were (and still are) multi-millionaires and totally focused on growing their wealth. Even at a young age, I understood that my family was quite different.

My uncles had nicknames for all 37 of the first cousins in my gene ration. To this day, I doubt they realize the profound impact they had on me by tagging me with the nickname "Jenny Who Ain't Gota Penny."

Can you imagine? Here I was, the poor, lonely only child of the lowest family on the totem pole, and tagged with a nickname that really cut deep.

I remember how upset I would get. I kept a penny in my shoe to show them that in fact I DID have a penny. It was a small thing, but it helped me feel better about my life.

One uncle went so far as to tell me that I wasdestined to be an alcoholic because it was in my genes. What kind of future was in store for me? I realized at a young age that failure isn't always about the person; it can simply be about their situa tion. I resolved to show ALL of them that I wasn't going to repeat history. I was going to do whatever it took to be successful and perfect in everything.

The Quest for Perfection

I was fortun ate enough to live next door to my wonderful grandparents. They were very faithful and took me to church nearly every day. Thanks to them, I developed a strong faith to help propel me during those formidable years.

I also started tagging along with my grandparents and all my uncles on their busi ness calls. I helped them clean their rental properties and worked at the family flower and garden business as well. I honed my work ethic and began to see what my life would be like without alcohol or the dysfunctional fighting. Learning the value of hard work instilled in me the desire to exceed in everything in an attempt to achieve perfection!

4

As a teen, I was a runner-up in the Miss Colorado competition . I was also a state champion in tennis and the youngest member of the Colorado Springs Symphony at 16 years of age, playing flute and piccolo. After graduation, I was accepted to Colorado State University in pre-med, though I changed to architecture, where I was the only woman in a class of 50-plus students.

I was the perfect daughter and never in trouble. Yet none of my efforts mattered, because my father still drank and was never involved in anything I did. How much more did a girl need to do to get her parents' attention and acceptance? Family members of alcoholics know that trying to be perfect is the way we think we can get our alcoholic family member to stop drinking.

Striving for perfection at a young age is why I still have so much drive in me today. Remember, motivation is an "inside job" and out of pain comes purpose. I was on the road to finding my purpose.

A purposeful direction on that road came from my husband, Brian. He gave me permission to take care of ME and not worry about pleasing my parents by attempting perfection.

Enter Mortgage Lending

How did this life then detour into mortgage lending? There I was, just out of college after studying for a degree in Architecture Design and Construction Engineering but not able to find a job in a male-dominated industry.

My mortgage lending career got underway in March 1983 after a chance interview and a cross-country move. It definitely paid off though! In my first 17 years in the mortgage business, I went from an entry level position to working my way up through sales management and finally to senior executive management.

Over the last 17 years (yes, I've been in this industry for just over 34 years!) I've worked directly with my clients by originating mortgage loans. Getting into the origination side of the business was the best decision I ever made. My income tripled, my quality of life expanded, and I showed everyone in my family that I could be successful and that Jenny did have pennies! I also overcame the stigma of this male-dominated industry to prove them wrong, too!

And I learned well from my uncles. In my thirties, I already owned several proper ties, was working smart, creating strong relationships, caring for others, and beat ing the odds by staying married and maintaining a strong faith.

Yet I still strove for that perfection and acceptance I so desired. Even today, I con tinue to have challenges. I avoid conflict like the plague and attempt to be as per fect as I can be. Therefore, I'm always leaning in to stay engaged in my practice and my person al life. It's what gives me my drive and passion for everything I do!

Today I'm at the top of my game. I've been recognized as one of the top 200 loan officers in the country and am in the top 1 percent of income earners. I've surpassed $1 billion in total production. Take that, you naysayers!

Fueled by Passion

Remember the learn, earn, and return stages I mentioned earlier? The return stage is a time that leads to rebirth and growth. It's a time for me to nurture the buds that spring into something wonderful in the next season. My hope is to fire you with the same passion that I feel for life and for this business, and that one of those wonderful buds that bloom next season will be you!

My driving force has always been my faith in God. He made me, as ordinary as I am, to do extraordinary things while I'm here on Earth! I love helping others realize their dreams and achieve success-as if they were my own.

I sincerely want your life to be as big as you can imagine. You don't have to com pare yourself to anyone but the you of yesterday. We all have the same 24 hours in a day to work with, and it's how you spend those hours touching other people's lives while quietly improving yourself along the way that counts.

Sure, I've had my burdens, lumps, and spiritual vine-pruning, and I'm sure to have more in the future. You will too! But it's how you assess, respond, and move for ward that will separate you from those who continue to allow the winds to carry them anywhere. Remember, when you fall, if you fall forward you're still moving! It's when you stop and give up that life takes the reins away from you.

These days, I'm blessed to not only be able to help people with their home-buying goals, but I get to help others through my speaking, coaching, teaching, and con sulting. I don't pursue a quality of life,I live a life of quality. My wish is to impart to you at least a few nuggets of my experience so that you, too, can look at life this way. You know, the great book Think and Grow Rich by Napoleon Hill isn't about money. It's about developing a rich life. Money does not define the core of who we are.

If you truly want to develop a rich life for yourself and your family, no matter what business or professional endeavor you tackle, I encourage you to ignite your life starting today. Right here and right now!

- Let your faith shine through. It's the driving force for your inspiration.
- Create a life and business plan that you can accomplish through systems to get more don e than you've ever imagined. Work on your plan DAILY.
- Don 't let anyone ever tell you what your life will be like-you are the driver. Lean in and make it happen. If I can do it, trust me, you can too!

- My father always said, "There are two ways to go out of this world- you can either rust out or wear out." Choose to wear out. Be an active partici pant in a life filled with joy and giving.

- Live like someone left the gate open!

- Love everyone, whether they lik e it and respond favorably or not! Ask yourself every day, "What more can I do to change or help someone else's life?" Sometimes it's as easy and simple as a phone call to say hello and bring a smile to someone 's day.

- Live a life of quality and you will be truly blessed.

- Move mountains.

My hope for all of you is that you awaken the spark inside you so you can move mountains and make your life grand.

✳ Ten Principles to Reach New Heights

> **The Big Idea:** Do the right things and do them consistently.
> You will catapult your practice to new heights.
>
> "Principles Live on...well beyond Wealth, Things, and Fame"
>
> -Anonymous

You can reach heights in your mortgage practice that so far you've only imagined. Even your wildest dreams are attainable-my career is proof of that.

But let's be honest: Reaching those heights doesn't just sort of happen. However, it's also not the impossible climb you might think. Your ascent starts with a simple axiom: Do the right things, do them consistently, and do them relentlessly. If you follow that, you'll be rewarded.

The one thing that drives me mad is when people "talk" about success, plans, sales, and making money, but they never actually do it. So, please, please, STOP TALKING. TAKE ACTION.

There are only a few principles you will need to follow to build an incredible future in this business. Every day, follow these ten basic principles to foster a successful, satisfying, and long-term career.

1)   Have a Burning Passion

You absolutely must have passion if you want to reach new heights of this business. That's what's really going to drive you to your success and legacy. People can hear that passion (or lack of it!) in your voice and can see it in your eyes.

Of course, it will take focused dedication and hard work on your part, but when infused with passion it will become much easier to reach your goals. To stretch for the heights, you'll have to do some things you aren't necessarily comfortable with doing right now. Perhaps you're not comfortable making ten phone calls every day to partners and clients, or perhaps you're not comfortable with going to net working events to meet new partners. I encourage you to persist at those things until you become comfortable with doing them. Once you're over that hump, your passion can shine through!

2)   Tackle Life with Drive

I don't want you to be the person who ends up saying, "I should have done this, I should have done more, I should have tried harder, I should have given more." Rather, I want you to have the confidence to believe in yourself. I want you to be the person who says, "I did all I ever wanted to do and more. I accomplished all I wanted to accomplish. I pushed myself to my full potential and achieved all of my goals." Otherwise, one day you may wake up and there may not be any more time for you to do all that you want to do.

Don't let time take your dreams away!

3)   Make a Plan, Develop Goals

You must have a vision and goals for your practice, or else it's just like looking through a muddy windshield. You can't really see where you're headed.

Having a clear vision will help catapult you to success. Don't try to develop the "perfect" plan. If you wait until everything in the plan is perfect, most likely you'll never implement it.

4)   Focuson Job One

To reach new heights, you must focus on the people, time, and activities that will advance your practice. First and foremost, focus on lead generation. Nothing else is important without enough business to help you reach your goals.

Stop being distracted by "shiny objects" and the "latestthing." Every day is a race to bring in more business, so make sure you're in the race and not just standing at the starting line. Here are some tips that I've found to keep you at the head of the race:

- Initiate contact with partners and clients via the phone. Make a commit ment to get on the phone every day, day after day, and call the people who will help you attract more business. Phone calls create momentum and keep the momentum going.

- Develop strong relationships by meeting with people one-to-one and face to-face. There is no substitute for this personal meeting; not email, not social media, not mingling at an event.

- Forge strong, mutually beneficial referral partnerships. Especially when you're starting out, this is where most of your business will come from. These partnerships will pay off handsomely over the long term.

- Create, maintain, and leverage a robust contact community-a contact database. When carefully constructed and maintained, this database will eventually become the heart of your practice.

- Show appreciation for anything and everything. This means writing and sending a thank-you note in appreciation for any meeting, any phone conversation, any referral, any favor. Thank-you notes can be backed up and followed by emails and personal videos-use your imagination when showing your appreciation! And be authentic and thoughtful in your gift giving and value-added propositions.

- If you focus on these essentials, your success is all but guaranteed. You'll continu ally get fresh leads and tons of referrals, and constantly grow your network and community.

5)   Take Action

The name of the game is action. A plan with no action behind it keeps you at the starting line. The more calls, meetings, and contacts you make, the bigger your chances for success, so do what you need to do to keep yourself top of mind with all your connections. Remember that sales is a contact sport.

Take action consistently and with discipline. Whatever works for you will work if you do it consistently. There is no magic bullet that replaces consistent action. If something works, do it again and again. The key is to never confuse activities with results. It's important to know exactly what works for you, or it's like eating soup with a fork.

Create checklists and have a defined process for everything. And by everything, I mean everything. This will double, triple, quadruple your productivity.

Take action intelligently. By that, I mean before you take any action or commit to any action, ask yourself these three key questions: Am I excellent at doing this? Do I absolutely love to do this? Does it make money sense for me to do this? If you answer "No" to two out of these three questions, don't do it!

Only take action on or do the things that you're absolutely excellent at. If you aren't excellent at something you should be doing to bring in business, find a way to become excellent. Hire out, staff up, and delegate everything else. Only do what you absolutelylove to do, and only do what makes money sense.

Find ways to separate yourself from other lenders and come up with fresh ideas to generate business. Do you need a new elevator speech? Try Ro ckstars in the Elev ator by Jim Beach on YouTube.

6)   Be a Professional

Conduct yourself and project yourself as a professional, not a run-of-the-mill com modity. Conduct your business with integrity, because people love to work with people they trust and it will show that you care about your image, your brand, and your industry. Be authentic. Learn who people are, not just what they do.

Make sure that you always act ethically. It's very important for you to have strong ethics and to know what lines never to cross, and to be aware when others might be crossing those lines. This is how you make a living; don't do anything to affect that.

Take your fiduciary responsibilities seriously. As you guide your clients through the loan and purchase process, their interests and their financial future should always be paramount in your mind. Direct clients properly and prudently to meet their financial goals, being careful never to focus on how the results will affect your income.

7)   Build a Team So You Can Excel

At each stage of your journey to the heights, you're going to have to let go in order to go higher. It might be scary or uncomfortable to hire an assistant and turn over to them some of the things you do, but it's a necessary step because you will reach a point in your business when you can't do everything by yourself. Without that additional help, you'll hit a brick wall, burn out, and give up on your practice.

Don't look at an assistant, or even a team of several people, as a cost. Having a team behind you gives you the opportunity to soar! While your assistant or team focuses on non-lead generating activities, you'll have the time to bring in more leads, more business, and more revenue. Delegating tasks to an assistant or team is a money maker for you if you use the time to bring in more business.

8)   Be a Life Learner

You should always keep educating yourself. Over the past decade, we've gone through some incredible turmoil and change in this industry. The profession has become much more demanding and complex, and it's becoming more and more prevalent that people in the industry need to be more educated and to elevate their professionalism. Higher education is going to be necessary to be licensed and recognized as a professional.

Learn from everyone in the industry, both from those who have been in the indus try for a long time and those new to the industry with fresh, new ideas. Meet periodically with other lenders in your area to bounce things off each other, share your challenges and successes, and create a mini-Master Mind Group.

Master new loan products. Look at a new product that you could sell and then master it so that you can help the type of client this product may be tailored for. Be creative-for example, a simple 25-year fixed rate loan can be sold as your SuperSaver Program.

9)   Improve Yourself

Every day, move yourself forward-your whole self. This is a vital aspect of work
ing on your business and yourself. Look at ways to improve your mind, body,
and soul.

Are you constantly improving your mind in a multitude of ways, not just in
ways related to this profession? Ask yourself, what am I going to do this year
to develop my talents and skills? Recommit to your career with a plan to get
smarter and bet ter, especially in the things you aren't excellent at.

Heck, have you always wanted to play the piano? Then learn how to play!
It's always about your growth and about mastering everything you possibly
can.

10)   Stop Talking About It

That's right-stop talking about it. Stop talking about what you're going to
do and get down to it! Don't keep saying, "We ll, I'll do such-and-such
someday." Or, "I think I'll try that someday."

Stop talking and take action! Someday is TODAY!

Jen's Jots

♦ There is a philosophy that I've followed for decades. In fact, I remind
myself of this philosophy during my daily affirmations. Follow this
philosophy and you'll be amazed at what you can accomplish:

If you do the things that are hard, life will be easy.

If you do the things that are easy, life will be hard.

- Les Brown

SECTION 2.
GOALS, PLANS, SYSTEMS

✳ Success Starts with a Clear Vision

> **The Big Idea:** Identify the passion that powers your practice so you can set a clear Vision for achieving your goals.
>
> "Fan the flame from within—from divine contract; not anger, not resentment."
>
> - Fabienne Frederickson

The first step to catapulting your success into the stratosphere is to know where you want to go and what you want to accomplish. In short, you need a vision before you start your journey.

If you don't have a vision and goals for your business, you'll be squinting through a muddy windshield. You might be driving along, but you really can't see where you're headed! You could be on the highway to success, but you also could be aiming for the ditch.

Let me ask you this: Could the reason that you haven't created a plan be because you think you need to create something as thick as a ream of paper? That is so not the way to go! If you wait until you have the perfec\ plan,you won't ever pur sueyour vision and realize the success that could be yours. Here's a little secret: *There is no perfect plan!*

What's Your Passion?

Being in this business starts with having a passion and having that passion drive you to be successful. People can sense that passion in your voice and see it in your eyes. It'll make you extremely successful in this business, no matter what anyone else thinks.

Are you driven to help people? Are you in business to help people realize their dream of owning a home, or are you in business to help people navigate a com plex episode in their lives? A little bit of all of these? Something else entirely? If your passion is just about the money, that will only get you so far. A passion is what powers you through each day, no matter how the day unfolds. For me, my passion starts with being a people person and having an innate drive to improve people's lives.

I'll betthat you have an underlying passion or passions right now. But I'll also bet that you haven't consciously identified those passions in your business. I know it took me a while to realize why I loved this business so much and why I wanted to be in it for my entire working life.

Embrace what your passion is for this business. That's the bedrock foundation on which you build your vision, and your vision will become your personal mission statement.

What is your passion? It will affect the market niche you fill and how you serve that market. It will affect the lines of business and product types you expertly deliver. Passion will enable you to deliver on your promises better than anyone else and to differentiate yourself.

Your vision is not really about reaching a certain income level-it's about fulfilling your passion. When you do that, you'll reach, literally, any income level you aim for.

Know the Numbers

You can print out your vision, frame it, and hang it in your office, but it's only decoration unless you translate this vision into action. You need goals, such as: What is your objective? What results do you want to achieve? What is your plan and purpose?

My belief is that setting goals and working toward those goals is not necessarily about reaching an endpoint. It's about working on the process of achieving the goals and living and breathing that process every day. If you make continual prog ress by following the process, you'll meet any goal you set for yourself.

When I first got into this business, we talked about goals, but we didn't really understand them. My thinking was, "Goals, Schmoals, who needs 'em?" Later on I realized that maybe I really did need goals, but I didn't know where to start! The first year that I decided to set goals for myself, I figured the best way to get goals into place was to simply write them down. So that's what I did. I remember that piece of paper very well! I wrote on it that my goal was to make $100,000 in the coming year. I simply divided it by 12 to get my monthly goal, and then I figured out how much I was earning on each loan. That gave me my plan: How many loans I had to close to meet my monthly and annual goals.

The problem with this was that I didn't write down any actionable items on how I was going to get there. I just wrote it down and said to myself, "Let it be written, let it be done!" Needless to say, I did not earn $100,000 that year!

At the end of the year, I told everybody that I wrote down my goals but I didn't achieve them. And everybody said, well, you can't just write down your goals, you must also tell other people about your goals. OK, got it. So again, I wrote down that I wanted to earn $100,000, figured out my monthly income goal, and how many loans it would take to make that goal. Then I told somebody about my

16

goals and said to myself confidently, "Let it be written , let it be said, let it be done." But guess what? Again, I didn't meet my goals.

That's when I realized that developing a solid business plan was the only way to get me to where I wanted to go, but more importantly, I had to act on the plan.

Let's look at an example of the process. Say you're closing five loans a month, and you set a goal to increase your closings to seven a month within the next six months. So that's the goal you start with: two additional closings per month.

This is where the process comes in. What is it you have to do to increase your closings? Do you have to cultivate new referral partners? If so, how will you do that? Do you have to create a more robust, daily phone outreach effort? Ifso, how will you do that? Does your contact database support a more robust effort, or do you first need to build it up? How many more referrals do you need each month to close two more transactions?

Is the goal of two more closings a month really the goal where you should start? Perhaps the basic goal you need to meet first is to cultivate four new referral partners a month for the next six months. After achieving that goal, then you can realistically aim higher-perhaps much higher-in the number of your monthly closings.

If your goal is to add four new referral partners a month for the next six months, then you'll need a process to use every day to work toward that goal. Identify the activities you'll dedicate specifically to finding those partners, working with them, talking to them, networking with them, and constantly following up with them. Work on the process of cultivating new partners each day, and this will lead to more referrals, which will lead to more closings per month.

Prioritize your goals. You can't tackle everything at once. If you bite off too much at once, you'll spin your wheels. To get momentum going, start with one or maybe just a couple of goals. Work on your process and plan to achieve that first goal. When you're moving forward smoothly and effortlessly, that's the time to think about incorporating another goal.

Measure

The last crucial step is to track your progress. You will need to set up a system to ensure you are following your plan, because how else will you know how much you've progressed sinee the start?

In the example I gave above, your aim is to cultivate four referral partners a month. Let's say you find that you actually need ten potential partners a month in order to cultivate those four partners withwhom you can do business. Track your success every month to ensure you're meeting ten potential partners and converting four of them to working partners.

You have to measure and adjust your performance to stay on track. If you don't keep checking, you'll drift off course. Think of an airliner flying cross-country for four or five hours-if it drifts off course by a degree or so every hour, it's going to be way off course at the end. The pilots (and the computers) check and adjust the plane's course constantly to keep it from drifting, and that's what you need to do to make sure you're working your plan to meet your goals.

Look at how you are spending your time now. Maybe even record what you do every day for a week so you have a better picture of exactly what you're doing and for how long. If you discover you're weak on lead-generation activities, look at where you can increase that time each day. It's also just as important to look at the activities that you can delegate to free up business-building time, or time wasting activities you can eliminate.

Consistency is Key

After 34 years in this business, I still set and work toward daily, weekly, monthly, annual, and even longer-term goals. I have a plan every year that includes goals to stretch for.It doesn't matter whether you're a rookie or a long-term veteran,you still need goals to drive you toward your vision.It all comes down to repeating the process month after month, and year after year:

- Find your passion.
- Set a goal.
- Make a plan to achieve that goal.
- Get to work on the plan.
- Stick to it, follow the process.
- Measure it.
- Reach the goal

Jen's Jots

- ◆ Set a vision and goals for what you want to accomplish in your life first.
- ◆ Revisit your vision and modify your goals every year.
- ◆ Meeting your goals is all about working through a process every day and taking baby steps forward rather than focusing on an endpoint.
- ◆ Prioritize your goals and track your progress.

✳ Getting Past the Plan

The Big Idea: *Implement your vision and goals with a business plan that drives how you will grow your practice.*

"The trouble with not having a goal is that you can spend your life running up and down the field...and never score."

- Bill Copeland

OK, so you have your vision and your goals. Now what?
The number one issue I hear when coaching or speaking is the difficulty that people have in following a business plan. They either don't have a solid enough plan,or they have a plan but it sits on a shelf,neatly tucked away in the credenza. I find this frustrating because it can be easily fixed.

Let's talk about how you get past the hurdle of waking up in the morning and knowing exactly what to do. You have to get past the point of just hoping that someone calls you with a referral,or going into the office and doing activities that don't generate leads or move the needle in your practice.

What you need is a blueprint for your practice. And it's a BIG DEAL! Just like you need a blueprint for using your time efficiently every day,you need a plan for how you'll generate business, how you'll ramp up your income, and how you'll meet your goals.

Let me give you an example. If you set out to build a house, would you start by getting a couple of truckloads of material at the home improvement warehouse, unloading the trucks, and just start building? Gosh,I don't think so. First you'd fig ureout your design and how to construct the basic bones of the house, and then you'd figure out your design for the interior and exterior, and how the finished house willlook. After you completed your plans, thenyou'd get the materials you needed to start building. Your business plan is based on the same principie.

Before we talk about the semantics of the plan itself, let's do a reality check, okay? People want to work with others they know, like, and trust-I'm sure you've already heard of this. Perhaps you've experienced it! I'd like to help you with this notion while you're creating your business plan. You see,we want to be the people who connect the dots for others-whether in business or working directly with clients. And we must make these connections explicitly. So sit back and look at your plan from the perspective of "Where do we want our business to come from?" and "What are the ways we will generate our business?" For example , if you want your business to come from realtors, what are some meaningful ways you can be in a realtor's world, ways that mean something for you as well as for them. Be honest with yourself: do you have the courage, the willingness, and the self-confidence to draw the links to the people we want to attract?

A plan is your personal guide on how you will increase leads and referrals, how you will develop and nurture profitable strategic relationships, and how your pro cesses will lead to helping more families get into a home. Everything else you do in your practice, every system and tool you use, are there to support these goals.

A business plan is like a seed. You can't just plant a seed and walk away, hoping at the end of the season that a huge, bountiful plant filled with fruit will be waiting for you. It needs your attention daily for water, sun, fertilizer, pruning, and care. It's the same for an effective business plan.

I cannot count how many times I've seen people in this business put plans together and then put them on the shelf. That won't work. You've got to track how well you're meeting your plan during your weekly blueprint time, your planning and review time. That way, you hold yourself accountable for the actions you say you want to take to meet the goals you set for yourself. Someday is today!

When you begin implementing your plan, the first thing you want to focus on is to only do things that you are absolutely excellent at. If you aren't good on the phone because that makes you feel uncomfortable,hire a dialer or a person who likes being on the phone. If you're better doing things in person, then do as many things as you can in person, such as networking, speaking to groups, or having small workshops or book clubs. If you're better at being on the phone and don't like going to networking events, then hire someone to be your business develop ment officer to go those events for you and speak on your behalf.

Know What You Want to Accomplish with Every Call and Meeting

Something a colleague recently shared with me is a reminder that we don't want to work with 100 pennies, or even 20 nickels. Perhaps our focus should be on working with 10 great dimes and 4 unbelievable quarters. Knowing what you want to accomplish begins with knowing who you want to accomplish your goals with. It also doesn't mean just keeping an overhead view and tallying your balance sheet at the end of every month. It's quite a unique combination thoughtful planning while remaining a visionary. Working your plan is a week-by-week, day-by-day, hour-by-hour endeavor.

Start with segmenting your time every day- also known as time blocking. Now, hang on! Don't close this book, stay with me! Time blocking can provide focus on the activities you want and need to accomplish during each time-compressed segment. I'll discuss the enormous value of time blocking and time compression in the next section.

In fact, there are several chapters in the next section all devoted to how you can wring maximum efficiency out of your time. The key is to not do things piecemeal, but to devote strict blocks of time to accomplishing defined tasks or like-activities. We do some of that naturally in our daily lives. For instance, when you return from the grocery store and put things away, you don't do it by taking one item out of the car, walking it into the house, putting it away, and then going back for another item. No, you bring in all the bags at once, you probably group things as you take items out of the bags, and then you store away all those similar items in the same location. That's the kind of efficiency you want to develop in your business activities.

As I mentioned in the previous chapter, you have to know exactly what numbers you need:
- How many referrals do you need?

- What are the sources of your loans going to be every single month? Where will your leads come from? Will 50 percent come from real estate agents? Will 20 percent come from financial planners? You need to know.

- What are your capture / conversion rates? (You may not have any idea what your rates are if you've never tracked these things. Just pick a num ber out of the blue in that case and then track your experience to figure out what your capture and conversion rates are.)

- How many loans do you need to close every single month?

When you know your numbers, your activities can be laser-focused! Without focus, you'll encounter difficulty reaching your goals.

For example, every phone call that you make should not be one and done- it should be a one and one. Know exactly who you want to talk to, and then ask for a referral or a new connection on every phone call. Utilize some scripting if you need to. Did you do that? Great, now you have another phone call to make. You can reach out to that person and schedule a one-to-one meeting for two to three weeks out.

If you get into the cycle of making appointments two to three weeks in advance, you're going to find very, very quickly that you're going to be booked with activities you love and that you are good at. More importantly, this gets results!

The key is to have a purpose for every meeting. You're following up because you have a system for following up, and you're scheduling the next meeting with that person right then and there while you're meeting with them. Don't wait to do it later or else you'll lose confidence to make that phone call to reach out to each other and schedule something. Just get it scheduled now while you're meeting them.

Keep working your plan daily, and you're going to find that you're busier than a bee. You won't have time to sift through Facebook every day. You won't have time to talk to clients who aren't going to be able to finance right now. You won't have time to talk to people who aren't going to refer business to you, and you may not even have time to go to broker opens. Is that something you do now and don't findbeneficial?

What's Your Plan?

If you don't currently have a plan or have never really thought about having a plan, today is the day to start putting one together! Why wait until tomorrow? Or the next day or next week? Let's build momentum today and keep that momentum rolling.

Like they say: You can make excuses or you can make progress. Your choice.

Jen's Jots

- ◆ Craft a business action planthat is your personal guide to increasing leads and referrals.

- ◆ Identify what you need to do every day to bring in new business and then get it scheduled!

- ◆ Everything you do should support your plan. Be sureyour plan is focusedonincreasingyourleads, referrals, strategic relationships,and production numbers.

✳ Be Clear and Fearless

The Big Idea: *Bring clarity to your efforts by focusing like a laser on the highest and best use of your time—the things you have to do to bring in new business and grow your practice.*

"Success does not come easily. Are you willing to pay the price?"

-Anonymous

Do you confuse activity with results? Rather than simply working longer hours, you should always be focused on making the highest and best use of your time to expand your practice.

Sad to say, most loan officers don't consciously focus their time on the actions that will move them forward. What drives you? Don't let day-to-day fears and anxieties override the focus and intensity you need to succeed.

Soft Light vs. Laser Focus

Imagine how it feels to be sitting back, comfortably reading in soft light. Kind of comfy and cozy, right? But that's not the feeling you want to power your plan! As Brian Buffini reminds us, you must focus like a laser on your most important activi ties. Don't spread out and dilute your energy like a soft-light bulb. Focusing like a laser comes down to consciously making small, intentional, but crucial choices every day that take you to the next level in your practice.

Ask yourself: What part of the day am I going to use to find business? How am I going to set up my weekly plan and schedule so I make sure I'm generating leads, finding potential clients, and working with referral partners to unearth new busi ness EACH AND EVERY DAY?

Be consistent. Every day, every week, every month.

You should be *prospecting* at least ten hours a week, which means you should be *prospecting* at leasttwo hours every day. Remember, prospecting isn't just making your daily phone calls-it's being in front of people, meeting with referral partners, having one-on-ones, or maybe even teaching a lunch-and-learn class. It's about business-to-business networking and marketing.

Those are the activities that will move you forward. Those are the activities that you MUST slot every day. They may require 20 percent of your time, but it is the most important 20 percent!

Approach your schedule with intensity and focus, instead of just simply putting in long hours while you convince yourself that you're leaning into your business.

Can Positive Fear Help You Focus?

These thoughts on fears are something I've learned from my mentor, Darren Hardy.

There are two different types of fear that we have in sales, particularly in lending. There is negative fear, which often blocks us-paralyzes us, really-from doing the things we need to do. And there is positive fear, which actually helps drive us because we fear the consequences of not doing the things we need to do more than we fear the possible rejection attached to doing what we must do.

Let's talk first about negative fear. This type of fear can misdirect your laser focus and cause you to dilute your attention. Instead of pinpointing your work for maxi mum effect, you look for ways to be active but unfocused. Negative fear trickles in and prevents you from taking action to introduce yourself to people. It blocks you from getting on the phone day in and day out, and it might even show up in your meetings with clients. You have that fear of rejection, or that fear of looking bad. It keeps you from doing the things you should be doing because the little voice in your head says, "You know, if you try that they might say no."

You could be turned down or rejected. You might even think you project a "salesy" image that no one likes. So rather than experience these negative feelings, you lose your laser focus or find other busy-work activities to fill in the time.

I've heard this from the loan officers that I coach, who say something like, "Well, I don't make phone calls to my database, because I don't know what to say. I don't want them to think that I'm pushy and I'm just calling because all I want is a referral."

The call is about getting or making a connection, not necessarily to get a referral; that will surely come later.

Negative fears can prevent you from doing the right things. I get it, you don't want to feel bad and you want to do the things that make you feel good. There's a problem with that though, a BIG problem. If you only do the things that make you feel good, you end up not doing what you *absolutely need to be doing every day* to accelerate your business.

Now let's look at fear from another perspective-what's called positive fear. I look at positive fear as motivating you to do the things you must do-even if youdon't like to-so youdon't suffer the consequences of leaving these things undone. For example, maybe it's the feeling you get of "I'm afraid that if my income drops, I won't be able to take care of my family," or, "I'm afraid that if I don't take care of my clients and give them a *Wow* experience they're going to do business with someone else."

This positive fear *propels* you to do the things that you normally wouldn't do or fear doing. The fear of not sustaining (or growing) your income is greater than the fear of going out and talking to people. You may even want to think of this in positive terms: "I can continue to support my family, and I can continue to bring in a high level of income if I get out there and make more connections, even though I find that hard to do."

It's a very small twist in thinking, but it's enough to help you remember and under stand that there's a difference between the fear that keeps you from doing some thing like making 10 outbound phone calls a day, which is a paralyzing fear, and the fear that motivates you to do that same thing every day, which is a pro pelling fear.

Think about the fears that paralyze you and the fears that propel you. You can even make a list of things you like to do and things you don't like to do, or a list of things that propel you and things that paralyze you. So if you're running into a problem of making phone calls to your database and it's paralyzing you, think about the flip side of your fear. If you make those calls, what will be the positive outcome?

Use these feelings to drive you and turn you from being someone who simply waits for business to come to them into someone who is actively going out and giving their all!

Circling Back to Clarity

Just what does this discussion about fear have to do with consciously focusing your time on the actions that will spark growth and maintain staying power in your practice?

Ask yourself: are you "inventing" tasks so you can trick yourself into thinking you are being productive? If so, circle back to consciously focusing on the things that are most important for growing your practice. Those are the activities that propel your business. Those are the activities you must tackle, no matter your fear.

Jen's Jots

- Consciously make small but crucial choices every day about the highest and best use of your time.

- Be consistent every day about how you schedule your time to prospect for business.

- Identify the things you absolutely NEED to be doing but maybe neglecting for fear of rejection or failure. Then use positive fear to propel you.

✴ Systems Are Your Salvation

> **The Big Idea:** Create and implement step-by-step processes, routines, and procedures in your practice to save time and energy and free up your time to bring in new business
>
> "Start by just sprinkling it in... don't worry about doing it all at once."
>
> - Jen Du Plessis

Loan officers lend to resist using systems to conduct their daily business. I know that's ironic, since loan processing and compliance with loan regulations are such systems-driven enterprises.

Let's be clear about this topic. Systems are those standard, organized processes, procedures, routines, and step-by-step methods thatyou follow in the daily opera tion of your practice. I am a true believer in creating and using a system for literally *everything* in my practice.

I preach endlessly about how crucial systems are in a mortgage loan practice. Creating and using systems and processes can improve your prospecting, mar keting, transaction processing, and most importantly, communications with your clients. Systems improve the quality and efficiency of everything and anything you do.

By following systems, you'll find yourself being more professional and you'll also discover that you're seNing your customers al a higher level of satisfaction.

As Michael J. Maher has shared, a SYSTEM is *Saving You* Stress, *Time, Energy, and Money*

If you don't have systems, you have leaks. Your prospecting system may be incomplete, or your marketing may be missing some important elements, or your loan transaction process may leave the customer in the dark if you don't have a communication system built in.

In short, without systems you may drop the ball in ways both small and large, in significant and imperative areas. Systems lock in habits and routines, with out which you may find yourself operating in an ad hoc manner. And there's no greater sin than "winging" it or just trying to replicate a procedure by memory.

27

Systems should be written, standardized, tested, and then revised and updated as you get more and more sophisticated in using them. Keep in mind that your systems will always go through revisions, so don't worry about being perfect. Try new things and update the old ways.

Where Can You Apply Systems in Your Practice?

Where can't you apply systems? You will save yourself time and energy, reduce your frustration, and give yourself loads more time for finding business when you apply systems across the board. Here 's just some of the places where you can apply a system:

- The loan / sales process and customer communication
- Internal office procedures
- Building and maintaining your database, your contact community
- Marketing plans and scheduling
- Outreach to existing clients
- Outreach to potential partners
- Your daily schedule
- Your syst e m for holding partner meetings

Let's Talk Examples

I'm so excited to share some of my systems with you-they're so powerful and yet v ery e asy to execute! These three systems (I have nine to tal) are the foundation of my practice. If you only do three, you have accomplished more than most.

Keeping in Touch with Potential Referral Partners. After I hav e an initial one on-on e meeting with a potential referral partner, I have a pr e plann ed scheduled system for reaching out to them seven times over the course of the next 70 days. This is my way of communicating with them to ensure that I've done my part to follow up with them after our meeting and to demonstrate my value.

After that series of communication s- and often before it ends- I can easily deter mine if we are ever likely to do business together.

My system involves social media outreach, send ing a relevant success stor y via e -mail , mailing a motivational book that appeals to the person, sending useful information via e-mail, and several phone calls. The point is, I have a system set up that preschedules each step and trigg ers remind ers to me. The materials are in place and the purpo se of each step is pr edetermined .

The key to any system such as this is to ensure that the receiver feels they are getting individualized, personal attention. I follow a set of "touches" within a sys tem that's designed to deliver value to the recipient, and I use automated tools to manage the process.

Perfect Loan Process. One of my mentors, Tim Braheem of Performance Experts, coined the term Perfect Loan Process. In my practice, we have a systematized process that details and tracks exactly what steps have been accomplished in the transaction process, *and* when and how we communicate to the customer as we complete each step. During the process, we have 71 points of communication during a single transaction. Yes, we've detailed 71 points of communication, which include emails, phone calls, text, video presentations, and more.

I started this process long before LoanToolBox to keep realtors and clients informed (truthfully-I wanted to keep that "at bay" in order to do my job!) before they called me asking for a status updates. In fact, my entire system was drawn out on legal size paper with my drafting tools because we didn't have computers back then. It felt as if the one who reaches out first and checks off all the "to-do" boxes first wins. It was, and still is, a game for me.

It's a thought-out, preplanned, systematized process, and though it may seem complex to you, it really makes our lives and practice *much* simpler. That's because we know nothing will ever fall through the cracks and we know we'll never forget a step. Our goal is to provide a superior customer experience, show our partners they can depend on us, and enable my team to be masters in their role in the process. The system helps us *anticipate* any possible outreach to a client and partner so we stay ahead of the curve.

A system will help prevent you from making a mistake that costs you money, will help you run things much more efficiently, and will prevent you from burning out. Your team, if you have one, will appreciate your system as well.

Road Map to Closing. Within my Perfect Loan Process we provide a checklist to our borrowers so that at each stage of the purchase transaction they can instantly see the progress of their loan, which we call a Road Map to Closing. It also helps trigger actions they need to take.

This system helps make the process smoother and more efficient. Just as impor tant, the system keeps the client informed so that they are much less likely to contact me with simple questions that are answered by the system. Instead of spending my time answering their questions, I can be spending that time focusing on lead-generating activities to bring in more business. That is a huge time-saver. Don't get me wrong, I love helping my clients, but truly, I can serve my clients bet ter when I can focus on my expertise, not on processing issues.

Where to Start?

I hope these few examples help you realize how valuable systems can be in your practice. Are you thinking about creating a whole bunch of systems? Well, don't do it! That's right, don't try to create everything at one time.

Think about what one system would make the biggest impact for you, your team, and your clients. That's where to begin.

Start with one, or think through and make an existing one better and more beneficial. Then test and use and revise that one system until you're happy with it before you move on to what you view as the next most important system for your practice. Dream big! Put everything into the system, even if you won't implement every step now.

And remember, these systems will always evolve. Even in my practice, I don't have every step in my Perfect Loan Process fully implemented, because I haven't found an appropriate tool or app to support some steps. Once you utilize a system for some time, you'll find even better ways to apply it for your success.

Keep thinking of ways to improve your systems and processes, and your investment in time and planning will pay off over and over again.

Jen's Jots

- Look at all aspects of operating your practice and how anything can be managed better through standardized systems.

- Create systems especially that help you serve your clients, or that you can use to increase your referral and customer base.

- Start by creating one system or improving a system you already have. Ask yourself how the system can be designed to save sanity, time, energy, and money.

SECTION 3.

TIME IS OF THE ESSENCE

✳ The Exhilarating Freedom of Time Discipline

> **The Big Idea:** You must be disciplined about how you use your time if you want to explode your business. You'll get more important tasks completed in less time, you'll generate more business, and you'll have more time for your personal life.
>
> "Discipline is the bridge between goals and accomplishment."
>
> -Jim Rohn

Let's face it: we all have the same 24 hours in a day. So why are some loan offi cers struggling along with two to three fundings a month while others can close 10, 15, or more? I've had lots of conversations with other top producers in the country, stretchingfrom New Jersey to California, and every one of them has one thing in common: they're very stingy about their time, They make sure that they get to the important things first and then everything else comes after.

In a word, successful top producers are disciplined about their time.

This chapter is a pep talk-well, really a lecture I guess-on being disciplined about how you use your time. In the following chapters in this section I'll talk more about *howto* getthe most from your time, but for now though, I want to talk about
why it's so important.

Discipline how you use your time* to *give yourself freedom. That seems like a contradiction, doesn't it? When you think about discipline, you probably think about being restricted, and when you think about freedom, you probably think about being able to do whatever you choose. So how does being disciplined about how you use your time make you liberated?

It's because lack of discipline actually leads to a lack of time! Be disciplined-I mean, really disciplined-about how you useyour time, and you'll get more done in less time, Be disciplined about what you're really supposed to be doing-pros pecting for new business, for example-and your income will certainly grow, Because of this new discipline,you'll have more money and more time *outside* of work, That's freedom!

Discipline is about taking advantage of efficiencies in your practice, Discipline is about doing first things first every day-tackling the things that will get you to your most important goal before anything else: moving the needle in your business or finishing a project. Discipline is about developing the work habits and routines that free up your time. Discipline is about being focused so you're not captured by the bumblebee syndrome, where you flit from pretty flower to pretty flower and scramble for the next new idea or deal.

Getting It All Done, and Then Some

In the classes and seminars I teach, people simply don't believe me when I tell them how much I accomplish in a day. Their first reaction is: That's not possible! How do you get it all done?

Was I some incredible loan officer dynamo right out of the gate my first year in the business? Gosh, no! But I learned how to develop efficiencies, how to focus on my top priorities, and how to schedule my time for my most important activities or tasks. And today, I manage five businesses, I'm a top-producing mortgage lender, I coach, I'm a motivational speaker, I'm a podcast host, and I have a real estate investment company.

In my non-work time I'm involved in competitive ballroom dancing and dance nearly every evening for several hours. I'm a wife, mother, and grandma, and cherish the time I devote to my family. I love to get in some competitive shooting, I work out, and I play tennis in the summer. I'm involved in church activities, and I get in some boating, canning, vineyard hopping, and charitable activities. I spend quality time with some close friends. Plus I read a lot of books.

When I describe all I do in a day, I see the class participants slumping in their seats, getting visibly tired! And frankly, I don't think they believe me, because they don't believe they can craft a life like that. But they can- and you can, too.

Focus on the Process, Not the End

I think the reason people can't envision themselves living a better life of quality is because they mentally try to leap from wh ere they are now to w here th ey want to be. It doesn't work that way. It didn't work that way for me, and it won't work that way for you.

What *will* work is developing the habits, routines, discipline, and yes, systems, to launch yourself on the *process* to your goals. But it takes some time. It's not going to happen overnight.

Launching yourself into great time compre ssion habits starts one habit at a time, and I'll talk more throughout this book about the nuts and bolts of maximizing your time discipline. Just as it's highly unlikely you'll fulfill a handful of New Year's resolutions all at once, you aren' t going to be able to put all of my tips into practice next week.

Start with one habit, one discipline, and break it down into bite-size, daily blocks to get started. Track and measure your progress. Remember, what gets measured gets improved.

Think of it this way: If you say, "I want to lose 30 pounds this year," where should you start? Well, losing 30 pounds is simply too big a goal to accomplish in one big leap. What you should do first is figure out how to change a behavior or several behaviors to begin the process of losing 30 pounds. For example, you might com mit to not snacking after 8:00 p.m., having a salad for lunch, and drinking five liters of water every day. But just those things and no others.

Once you've done that, track and measure those three commitments on a daily basis. Did I have a salad today? Did I drink five glasses of water? Did I avoid hav ing a snack after 8:00 p.m.? And if those are the things that you feel are going to help you lose 30 pounds, then start. Start with easy-to-implement tasks first so you can gain momentum. NOT 20 things, but just three things that will help you stay motivated to get to your goal.

Once you've mastered those habits, then you can introduce new habits. And again, compare this to New Year's Day when maybe you've made all sorts of resolutions. You want to spend more time with your family, lose weight, work out more, get a promotion, travel more-you've got all these goals that are absolutely too difficult to achieve all at one time. You have to break these goals down into daily activities that you measure and that you grade yourself on how well you did. That will help you get better at what you do. That's how I mastered the use of my time over my career, and that's what has allowed me to be more efficient and effective. Oh, I fell off the bandwagon every so often! This is hard! But it can be done, just like losing weight.

It didn't happen in the beginning for me. Understand that you have to take baby steps before you get to where you're disciplined and focused. We'll delve into how to do that as we move along.

Get Segmented

Do you allow your in-box to manage your to-do list? By that, I mean does what ever the in-box tells you to do, based on everyone else's schedule, control your day? Why does someone else get to decide what your priorities are? Rather than you working at your three major goals for business that week, does your in-box decide for you? Leave your computer off and say to yourself, "What are the three things I need to do today to accomplish my one big goal?" Don't turn on your computer the minute you walk into your office and then have your time driven by your e-mail.

Get your priorities done first, and then the rest of your work can be done later. That is the only way you're going to discipline yourself to accomplish your goals.

Without discipline, when you get to the office your time and attention will get broken up into little, unrelated pieces. You can easily get distracted by the per son who asks if you have a quick minute. Or by answering the phone right now instead of waiting and calling people during a time block after listening to your messages all at one time. Or first dealing with transaction issues instead of mak ing outbound phone calls.

Don't be a one-tasker. Don't do one task in one area, then do one task in another area, then another type in a third area. That's like putting away the laundry one article of clothing at a time. When you empty the dryer, would you take one item, fold it or hang it up, then immediately carry it to the bedroom before going back and doing that with a second item? Then a third?

Of course not. But I'll bet you *constantly* follow that model at work. You do, don't you? I can practically see that look of realization on your face. You put away one article of clothing at a time instead of taking care of the whole laundry basket in one trip. (Well, you know what I mean. You aren't doing laundry at work, but you're using the system I just described to get your work done!)

Discipline Yourself or Someone Else Will

There are many, many ways to get disciplined on how you use your time and most importantly, focusing on your priority tasks.

- You can schedule your time in blocks and compress like-activities into each block-a technique called time compression. This is something I learned from one of my mentors, Darren Hardy, founder of Success maga zine and host of DarrenDaily, a daily mentoring program.

- You can blueprint your day and week so you always know what and when you have to accomplish.

- You can redirect incoming demands into the appropriate time block so that you're never distracted from the tasks, activities, projects, and goals you should be working on.

- You can focus on playing offense instead of defense; that is, prospecting for business and generating leads instead of answering incoming status calls.

We'll discuss each of these ways to discipline yourself in the next several chapters.

The bottom line is that if you're going to get where you want to go, you have to be great at disciplining your time. And there's no wishing you could be more disciplined-you have to work on the process every single day.

No, I've never been in the Marines, and I'm not Sergeant Du Plessis, getting up in your face and screaming at you to discipline yourself so you can achieve your vision. (Although if you want to schedule a time to meet me at my office, I'll be happy to do that!) If you put in 10 or 12 hours a day at the office, day after day, but aren't focused and disciplined about your time, well, I maintain you aren't really working all that hard. You're putting in 50 or 60 hours a week but treading water.

If you apply time compression with consistency, you can accomplish five times more than the average loan officer in a year. Ten times more! Would you like a life in which you were producing five times more loans a month? Ten times more loans a month? All while having more time than you do now for your family and friends and doing the things you love to do? Yes, I do believe you would! The key is to embrace the exhilarating freedom of time compression.

Jen's Jots

♦ Start with one type of task, such as returning phone calls, and block out one hour every day for this task.

♦ Track and measure on a daily basis this new time habit and routine you're trying to follow.

♦ Look at how your day unfolds now. Work on grouping like tasks together to compress these activities into a scheduled time block.

♦ Now add another type of task (such as loan analysis) and block time daily where you will do nothing but this task during that time.

✳ Crunch Time

> **The Big Idea:** You can control your schedule and be super-productive by compressing like activities into defined time blocks. "Make sure you have family time...always."
>
> -Anonymous

Ugh. For most people, it's like holding their nose and swallowing the awful-tasting medicine. There's just no sugar-coating what I'm going to talk about in this chap ter, and that's time compression, which is also called time blocking. Aaagghhh! There,I said it. Time compression, time blocking. (Okay,okay, remove your hands from over your ears. You have to listen to me.) Your practice and your income will thank me for what I'm about to tell you.

It doesn't matter what name I use, people react viscerally to the thought of time compression or time blocking to manage their day. I didn't like it at first either, believe me, and my team fought it, too! But what we found is that with time com pression, we are actually able to seNe our clients better. We are happier because we have more life to live AND we achieve our goals every year. In fact,we reach our goals no matter what is happening in the wider economy with rates or home values.

Using time compression provides us with a schedule and business we can count on.It is the ultimate productivity power tool.

Why not develop the time compression habit right now? If you're new in the busi ness or have been in the business for a while, and you just can't seem to get everything finished thatyou wantto accomplish each day, why not consider some time blocking/compression?

There is one very important key that will help make time compression successful for you. First,you need to know what *your* role is and what is most important for you to do each day so you can make the most efficient use of your time.

There is so much that you need to do in a day. You need to first carve out when you should be doing the most important parts of your job, then you need to schedule when you should be doing the activities that are important but do not directly lead to generating new business. And please, always focus on business building activities from 9 to 5. That is not the time to be working on your budget or printing flyers for next week. Do that later if you have to do it yourself.

With time compression, you create blocks of time exclusively for business build ing-for lead generation, for meeting with referral partners, or for moving your practice forward.

Recognize what your most important role is, then block your time to accomplish that role. Make sure you put those pieces into your daily calendar...FIRST! After you have these blocks in place in your schedule, you must discipline yourself to work on ONLY those activities reseNed for that block.Nothing else.

The blocks are sacred. Again, work on only those activities reserved for each block, nothing else. You'll compress the amount of time you spend on those activi ties overall. When you group the activities together, you get more efficient and effective at accomplishing them.

Here's a typical weekly time-blocked or time-compressed schedule.

	20 Monday	21 Tuesday	22 Wednesday	23 Thursday	24 Friday
7:00 AM	Workout Daily Plan & Review Affirmations	Workout Daily Plan & Review Affirmations	Workout Daily Plan & Review Affirmations	Workout Daily Plan & Review Affirmations	Workout Daily Plan & Review Affirmations
8:00					
9:00	1st and 10s - PROActive 1	1st and 10s - PROActive 1	1st and 10s - PROActive 1	1st and 10s - PROActive 1	1st and 10s - PROActive 1
10:00	1:1 or Client Meeting		1:1 or Client Meeting		1:1 or Client Meeting
11:00					
12:00 PM	Lunch with A+/A	Visit Client and Partners	Lunch with A+/A	Visit Client and Partners	Lunch with A+/A
1:00					
2:00	1:1 or Client Meeting		1:1 or Client Meeting		1:1 or Client Meeting
3:00 4:00	Customer Service	Customer Service	Customer Service	Customer Service	Customer Service
5:00	Blue Print Time	Blue Print Time	Blue Print Time	Blue Print Time	Blue Print Time

Work with Intentionality

Working with a time-compressed plan is based on the principle of intentional intervals. You work with laser focus on one type of activity and complete those activities in a shorter period of time. You *choose* to work on only those activities.

Do this, and you'll be able to dedicate 100 percent of your time and energy to each interval in your schedule. Your laser focus will overcome the natural ten dency to let your focus slip away and then work at 50 percent (if that!) of your capacity.

Look at intentional intervals this way: If you're watching television, are you *actively* choosing what you're watching? When a show ends, how do you decide what to watch next? Are you truly intentional about your choice, or will you simply watch what's served up for you?

During your day, are you *actively* choosing exactly what you will work on next? Or are you reacting to what's served up for you by someone else, by a phone call or by an email? You don't have a lot of time to accomplish what you need to do each day, especially if your goal is to double or triple your income, so you *must* be intentional about how you block your time and what you work on during each block.

Getting Scheduled

When you set up your calendar to compress your activities, your goal, first and foremost, is to block time specifically for lead-generating activities: daily phone calls, meetings, and networking. Follow this principle and it will virtually guarantee you success. Focus on lead-generating activities by blocking out time in one- and two-hour segments where you will NOT be putting out fires in the office.

Create your complete weekly calendar by considering the activities you have during any given week. Here is a sample list to get you thinking- this is the order I use to create my time-compressed schedule.

- Family Obligations
- Exercise
- Personal Growth & Development
- Blueprint/ Planning Time
- Team Meeting
- Office Sales Meeting
- Processor Meeting
- Daily Phone CallsRealtor Meeting
- B2B Meeting (attorney, financial planner, etc.)
- Visiting Client/ Marketing
- Initial Client Meeting
- Loan Applications
- Attending Closings
- Networking Event
- Networking Luncheon
- Training Class

- Seminar (realtor, client)
- Wiggle Room/White Space
- Loan Analysis & Research
- Transaction Management
- Writing Thank-you Notes
- Administrative Work

Print a weekly calendar and begin entering your obligations in this order:

- **Family obligations** (birthday parties, dinner with significant other, events).

- **Personal time** (reading, researching, exercise, spiritual, motivational).

- **Regular company obligations** (sales meetings, processor meeting, team meeting).

- **Business time** (administrative tasks (budget, reports], creating marketing/ flyers, open house flyers, review of goals, thank you notes).

- **LGA Daily Phone Calls!!!** (plan one hour per day and schedule for two different time slots [for example: Monday, Wednesday, and Friday, 9:00 a.m. to 10:00 a.m., and Tuesday and Thursday, 4:00 p.m. to 5:00 p.m.]).

- **LGA Meetings** (real estate agent, referral partner, luncheon, initial client and loan application [plan two hours for each meeting as this will provide you with wiggle room]).

- **Scheduled closings**

- **Transaction management** (loan analysis, client communication and follow-up, initial client referral calls, guideline review, etc.).

- **Business time** (administrative tasks [budget, reports], creating marketing/ flyers, open house flyers, review of goals, thank you notes).

You know the expression: Don't let your schedule control you, you control your schedule. That is exactly what this system empowers you to do. I understand that life happens and you may get pulled away-this IS the mortgage business after all. Just try to remember to "replace it, don't erase it." What do I mean?Well, when something unexpected comes up, don't delete the time blockyou were in; instead move it to another time that same day. Consistency isn't catching up several days later with a longer time block,but I'll discuss this concept in a later section.

Start today by building "blocks" in your schedule so you can compress like-activ ities into pre-scheduled time slots. If you've never followed this system, start with the most important blocks for lead-generating activities and prospecting for cli ents. From there, widen out to the whole day,following the bullet pointsI've listed.

Once you start using this system to control your schedule, what you'll really con trol is your time, income, and success.

Jen's Jots

- ♦ Control your daily schedule by creating intentional intervals during which you work on only one type of activity.

- ♦ Focus first on separating lead-generation activities into distinct blocks of time.

- ♦ Create a weekly calendar to schedule time blocks for all your obligations: family time, personal growth time, lead generation, closings, transaction management activities, and business tasks.

- ♦ Replace time blocks,don't erase them.

✳ Developing Great Habits

> **The Big Idea:** Develop habits and routines for everything you do to get more done in less time.
>
> "We are whatwe repeatedly do.
> Excellence, then, is not an act, but a habit"
>
> -Aristotle

To be effective in personal management means developing habits, routines, and behaviors that enable you to get more work done in less time. Habits and routines are part of life. Some are developed subconsciously,like how you get ready for work in the morning, while others you may have just fallen into. Or perhaps you've consciously developed a routine for specific aspects of your life. You probably do the same things in the same order every day so you can save time, and if your routine is disrupted for any reason it takes you longer to get ready.

I'd like to discuss a few habits you maywantto consider developing that will help you accomplish tasks with greater efficiency. Developing and maintaining habits and routines for everything will reduce the time it takesto complete various tasks.

I'vetalked before about how I fit in everything that I do into a day.With a handful of businesses to run and an uncompromising attitude about spending time with my family, friends, and the many hobbies I love,I need to have good habits and routines. I wouldn't really be in the position I'm in if I didn't cultivate and follow these habits.

Setting Up Your Day

Your morning routine sets the tone for the entire day. Get into the groove of fol lowing morning habits to get your day started, and you've already won a huge battle. Every morning I get started by following the advice of Hal Elrod, author of *The Miracle Morning,* who encourages early rising and a routine that mentally prepares you for the day.

While Elrod suggests getting up at 5:00 a.m.,I find that 6:00 a.m. works for me. I stick to getting up at 6:00 a.m. every day and execute one hour of Elrod's SAVERS Program. (Silence, Affirmations, Visualization, Exercise, Reading, and Scribing (journaling)). These simple 6 habits prepare me for the day. You don't have to take a full hour, but that's what works for me. The critical piece is to carve out time for mental preparedness each day.

Compartmentalize Similar Activities

Recognize and take advantage of efficiencies in your mortgage practice. The more that you can do like-minded activities at the same time, the more efficient you will get. Utilize time to the best of your ability.

For example, if you're looking to price a loan, price a bunch of loans at one time. Don't price one loan, then work on the checklist of documents that you still need from that client, then do some other part of the process on that loan. It's very inefficient to perform multiple steps on one loan in a linear fashion. Price several loans at one time to compress the time you spend doing that task. Get into a habit, a routine, of grouping like activities. You may even be able to skip a step because the loans may be similar with the same circumstances.

You can apply the same principle to every aspect of your practice. Whether it's meetings, completing a loan analysis, or phone calls, if you can group these tasks together, you're going to be much more efficient and you're going to be able to create habits faster.

Meeting can be the worst efficiency and time wasters, not because you are meeting a potential client, but how they are scheduled and leave you running from one meeting to another across town. Please don't meet someone, come back to the office, go out and meet with another person, then come back to the office again. Try to stack the meetings one right after the other at the same location, leaving some white space in between appointments so you can record an audio debrief about the meeting, write a thank-you note, or do some follow up from the meeting (emails, introductions, etc.).

(By the way, initiating and completing tasks *immediately* after a meeting is another habit that will make your life much simpler and more efficient.)

Team Aspect

Be sure your team- or maybe your assistant if you have one- is also following efficient habits and routines. I was finding that when a new contract came in, for example, my assistant was working on one loan all the way through to submission to compliance, leaving other files sitting and not progressing rather than segmenting her day and doing similar activities together.

Let me explain in further detail. You could make phone calls with no interruptions from 9:00 am -10:00 am while at the same time, your assistant could be in quiet time. When you are both finished, you can now take 10-15 minutes to debrief one another before moving on to each of your next time blocks. This time you may be reviewing your business plan while your assistant is doing follow up from your earlier calls. If you don't coordinate your time blocks, you may not find any time to meet during the course of a day.

Additionally, this provides a higher level of customer service, experience, and satisfaction. Clients won't be waiting for a response because you "haven't had a chance to talk to your assistant/processor/underwriter yet."

Finite Number of Days

Habits are incredible. At the end of the day, you could find yourself having done more in a day than most people will do in the entire week. Every minute, hour, and day counts. Think about it-we don't have that many days to actually do work. Darren Hardy explained this one day on his DarrenDaily video podcast. Hang on, because this may hurt!

If you are 20 years old today, you'll have 10,800 days that you'll be waking up to go to work to make a difference-if you work until you're 65. If you're 30, your number of work days is down to 8,400. If you're 50, you've got just 3,60 0 days of work left!

You must make the most of your days! Period. Bottom line. Pay attention to your use of time and only take on tasks that are important, do them well, and do them only in the most efficient way you possibly can. Challenge yourself to think through your decisions and ask, "Is this the most efficient way I could be doing this task?"

When you follow great habits, you'll create a life of quality for yourself. You're going to have a much broader life that allows you to reduce the stress this indus try creates, enjoy what you do, and allow for your passions to be realized,

Jen's Jots

- ◆ Consciously develop and follow habits and routines to be more efficient in your work.
- ◆ Always group similar activities to take advantage of efficiencies.
- ◆ Segment the activities of everyone on your team, including you, into the same time blocking to serve each other and clients more efficiently.

✳ Build Each Day with a Blueprint

> **The Big Idea:** Blueprint your plan of attack every day the day before.
> Set yourself up to succeed every day by being prepared and
> professional.
>
> *"Plan your work ..work your plan"*
>
> *-Anonymous*

Let's dive right in to one more aspect of how you cancontrol your daily schedule. So far we've talked about the importance of being disciplined about using your time and about working in concrete blocks of time so you can compress your work and get more done. Now let's talk about thinking ahead every day, or what I call *blueprint* time.

Think about the blueprints for a house that show the framework that supports the finished product. Just like real blueprints, if you create a blueprint ahead of time for the framework of your day,you'll wind up with a beautiful, finished design.

Blueprinting One Day Ahead

What I mean by blueprinting your day is to set aside some time each day to review, prepare for, and mentally walk through your next day's activities. When you do this is not as important as making sure you do it. I find that it works best to do this in late afternoon, but you should find a time that best fits your way of working.

The blueprint time is about setting yourself up to succeed at whatI call the six P's: Planning, Preparing, Practicing,Presenting, Producing, andPhollow-up. (Hey,I had to be phonetic about phollow-up, or else my creative listwouldn't be so creative!)

During your blueprint time,you plan and prepare for the day and your scheduled activities, you practice what you might present in a meeting, you think ahead to what you want to produce during each activity on your calendar, and you antici pate any follow-up actions.

Let's say, for example, that you're going to be meeting with a real estate agent partner the next day. You mightwant to make sureyou have your brochure on an upcoming class or seminar that you're going to be putting together. Or perhaps you're at the stage of showing your potential value to them, so you

46

want to pull together some of your recommendation letters to share with them or the success stories your clients have written about you. You want to make sure you have all your materials in hand and ready to go. Walk through in your mind what it is you want to talk to them about-what do you want to accomplish at the meeting? Really preplan in your mind how that meeting's going to go.

Likewise, what if you have a presentation scheduled? Do you know how many people are coming? Do you have your presentation ready? Is it on your com puter? What if the computer doesn't work withthe projector at the venue? Have you backed up the presentation on a USB drive? What if neither of those options works? Have you printed out your presentation notes so thatyou candeliver your presentation without having slides available?

So think about all the variables.

What about a planned meeting with a client? Perhaps you're having a discovery meeting, as I call them, which is a meeting where you're meeting a client for the first time to discuss their situation and discover the best options available to them. Do you have your collateral available? Have you done some preliminary research so you're well prepared as a professional loan originator? Do you have
your mortgage total cost analysis ready? Have you checked the markets? Do you know exactly where rates are today, where they might be heading, and what the trends have been?

This blueprint time is really important to ensure thatyou are the best that you can be. You won't be frazzled because you forgot something. You won't look unpre pared because you waited until the very last minute to print out materials only to discover that the computer isn't talking to the printer.

Set aside some blueprint time every day. Plan and prepare for your next day or two days' worth of activities. That way, you'll look and represent yourself as the professional you are.

A Metaphor for Planning Ahead in Your Practice

Don't just spend time reviewing your blueprint daily;you should also look ahead to see how today has impacted or willimpact your week, month, and year.

Think about your time and the highest and best use of your time. Ask yourself: How am I going to set up my weekly plan and schedule so that I make sure I'm generating leads, finding potential clients, and working with referral partners to unearth new business each and every day?

Where do you want to be spendingyour time? How can you set up your day, the week, and the next month to generate new business? And how can you set up your time to serveyour clients better?

Plan your schedule with intensity and focus. Don't simply put in long hours while you convince yourself you're leaning into your business. Think. Think. Think.

Jen's Jots

♦ Set aside some time each day to review, prepare for, and mentally walk through your next day's activities.

♦ Ask yourself what you want to accomplish at meetings, while networking, or during your daily outbound phone calls.

♦ Prepare ahead of time to eliminate the unexpected, which could make you stumble in your routine and/or in achieving your goals.

Here are some of the activities and tasks you can check and prepare for during your blueprint time:

- Review your schedule for tomorrow.
- Review your schedule for the next few days.
- Confirm your appointments and meetings.
- Make sure you have all the necessary tools you need for your upcoming appoint- ments:
  - > Calculator
  - > Computer, with power cord
  - > Business cards
  - > Nametag
  - > Brochures
  - > Flyers
  - > Give-away items.
  - > Free drawing item.
  - > Basket'bowl for collecting cards.
  - > Food arrangements (if you are doing broker opens or lunch-and-learns)
  - > Contact information for the people you are meeting
- Handouts for presentations.
- You've practiced your presentation.
- Breathe. Meditate. Workout (or dance like I do).
- Think through how you would like an upcoming meeting to go. Perhaps you have a meeting with a referral partner or client. What is your goal for the meeting? What will you tell them about your business and what makes you different? What do you want to find out about them? If it's a potential referral partner, do you have some thing specific in mind to help their business grow? How will you present that? How will youcommunicate after the meeting? What is your follow-up plan?
- Review what you accomplished today and what needs to be done tomorrow; that is, your TO DO list. Keep in mind what needs to be time blocked vs. what can be done in a few minutes.
- Who will you be calling during your outbound phone time? Do you have their num bers available? What will you be talking about? Have you reviewed notes from previous calls so you can ask about things important to them?
- Do you have enough gas in your car? (I have been late more than once because my car was extremely low on gas and I hadn't planned for gas station time.)
- Is there anything else that might affect your schedule? Road construction?
- Unfamiliar route for which you need to program your GPS?
- Emails introducing partners to one another and clients.

Get organized. Take the time every day to plan your activities so you can repre sent yourself and your practice in a totally positive and professional light. Even during blueprint time, consider compartmentalizing like-minded activities.

✳ The False Allure of Balance

> **The Big Idec:** *Don't strive for that illusive concept of balance. Use this time compression technique so you can dedicate 100 percent of your attention on whatyouneed to accomplish and work more efficiently.*
>
> *"Try Intensity & Focus..instead of long hours"*
>
> *-Anonymous*

I don't believe in balance. I don't believe in the concept of balance. I don't believe in 'linding" balance. I do believe that you can find peace, joy, and contentment, but just not through the myth of balance.

The thought of "'balance" holds out a false allure for most everyone. You try to "balance" many different kinds of tasks at one time at work, with family, and in life. But what you get is a frustrating, anxiety-inducing daily hustle and flurry. When you try to wedge in too many different types of efforts into the same time block, you get rushed and sloppy and then you start sacrificing more time from family and life to be more successful. And there goes your attempt to find balance.

Don't misunderstand, you can be super-successful at work and at home and still have time to do the things you love to do. But it's not because you'll find "balance." Instead, develop ways to work at 100 percent of your capacity and attention on the customer or person you're helping or the tasks and projects you're working on. Focus your efforts by practicing time compression. You'll complete your work more efficiently, your business will get better, and the time you have for your family and friends and life will be enriched.

Doesn't Balance Mean You're Only Functioning at 50 Percent?

When I think about balance, it makes me think of an old-fashioned hanging balance scale. When the scale is balanced, there is equal weight in both trays. But of the total weight in those two trays, only 50 percent of the item is being weighed.

Just like the balance scale, when at equilibrium you might feel like you're balanced, but I believe you're truly functioning at 50 percent of capacity. You could be functioning at 100 percent of your capacity by focusing like a laser beam on the task at hand during the specific time you have blocked on your schedule to accomplish that task.

Don't Worship at the Shrine of Instant Service

In the mortgage industry, we're sales and service people. We inherently want to service our clients as quickly as possible. I guess at some point everyone in the industry made a pilgrimage to the *Shrine of Instant Service*. It's where we paid homage to the deity that tells us we must talk to the client the instant they call, no matter what else we're doing. Or the deity that tells us we won't be worthy unless we're juggling five unrelated tasks at once on five different loans.

I'm here to tell you that you've got to change your religion.

It's a detriment to your practice to try to serve a client as quickly as possible no matter what the circumstances. It's a detriment to your practice for you or any of your staff to try to wedge together unrelated activities or tasks on different loans so that you can "balance" the progress you're making in the loan process.

Picture this scenario: You're driving to a meeting, or you're in a training seminar, or you may have been able to block out time to attend a parent-teacher conference at your child's school. A client or potential calls and wants to have a conversation about their loan, or about applying for a loan because they're buying a house, or about refinancing.

Do you take the call right then and attempt to engage in a productive conversation?

No. No. No.

Given the circumstances, are you going to be able to *really* engage 100 percent of your time and attention on the client? No. Are you going to be able to answer their questions in the detail they deserve? No. Are you going to be able to care fully note or remember all of the follow-up actions you might need to take as a result of the call? No.

Worse yet, what percentage of the attention you're supposed to be giving to driving, to your meeting, or to your kid's teacher just went out the window? You will more than likely have to double back later and have another call to figure out what you missed on the first call. This is more time that's lost!

Think of the folks you see in the grocery store. You know the ones (not you, of course!) who are on the phone, while pushing a cart with a child, while looking for the items they want. They're looking, they're talking on the phone, they're pulling things off the shelf, putting them back, trying to keep their kid under control, bending down, talking, searching the shelves. Are they really giving full attention to anything they're doing? Not by a long shot!

Remember the image of that frazzled shopper in the grocery store the next time you're tempted to answer the phone and try to offer service to your client right then and there, no matter what else you're doing. Not a pretty picture.

If you do take the call, by the time you finish your conversation you can't remember all of the details. You end up having to call the customer back and ask your questions again, or try to disguise the fact that you need to ask the same questions by beating around the bush with other questions.

Schedule and Manage Your Client Service

A key benefit of using time compression is that it enables you to serve your customer *better,* get your work done more efficiently, and cut down the time you ultimately spend on this task. There is a way to manage and schedule these calls and conversations.

Slot these kinds of conversations into the time block that you have reserved for having these calls and for delivering this customer service.

During the day, if you're not in a position to give the customer 100 percent of your time and attention, either don 't answer the phone and let the call go to voicemail, or answer and tell the caller something such as this: "I answered your call because it is very important to me. However, I'm about to go into a meeting right now, and am not able to give you my full attention. I want to spend the time to help you and answer your questions. Would it be okay if I called you between 3:00 p.m. and 5:00 p.m. today when I am in front of my computer and can deliver 100 percent of my attention to serving you?"

Now, between 3:00 p.m. and 5:00 p.m. is the time block that I generally reserve to take care of these types of calls and perform this service. And because I have that time reserved, I can compress the time I spend on these calls and get them done well andefficiently.

You're skeptical. I understand. If you get a call from a client at 11:30 a.m., you feel duty-bound to have a conversation right then, not a few hours later. It's a natural instinct. It's what you learned on your pilgrimage. But that behavior just doesn't enable you to move your practice forward. And it probably doesn't enable you to provide world-class service to the customer.

I've never had a client say, "No, I don't want you to dedicate all of your attention to serving me. I want you to talk to me now when you're distracted or trying to do something else."

Don't be afraid to ask them to schedule a better time to talk, and then give them a time block during which you'll call them back.

Make sure you get that last point. Give them a time *block* during which you'll call them back. Not a *specific time.*

Have you ever had your mind wandering during a meeting or application, thinking about the low appraisal that just came in, or an email from a client with more ques tions, or the client you forgot to call back at 1:30 because you got behind while in a meeting with another person? I bet you have, and I have too. This situation isn't serving anyone fully. You aren't getting back to or addressing the low appraisal so everyone is waiting on you, the client on the other end of the email is becoming impatient because you haven't responded as quickly as you normally do, and you may have lost the other client because you didn't call back when you said you would. All of this over part of the syndrome I call "overserving."

As a sales person, you're eager to please. Your natural tendency is to say some thing like, "Let me call you at 4:00." But then 4:00 o'clock rolls around , and you 're tied up, and it becomes 4:05, then 4:10, or you have an overlapping call that's gone on, and now it's 4:15. And now you don't look very professional. Inform them you'll call them back during the block during which you know you'll be making calls. Carve out an *intentional interval* for providing customer service on your daily schedule, and then slot the call into that intentional interval.

By following this system you'll always have the time you need to truly dedicate 100 percent of your attention to your client's questions and needs. You'll get all the details nailed down and you'll deliver service that customers will rave about.

Oh, and you'll stay sane. And you'll get more accomplished in less time. And you'll find you'll have more time to enjoy your life and your family and your friends.

Now that's balance!

Intentional Intervals for Your Team

This principle of dedicating 100 percent attention also holds true for your team members who work in areas such as processing. So if a team member is pricing a loan, or reviewing tax returns and paystubs, or trying to plug information into the loan operating system, or LOS, then ideally they should be doing all the pricing in a batch, all the reviewing in a batch, all the plugging in a batch.

They also should slot particular activities into particular time blocks. If they're flipping back and forth, getting distracted by other team members interrupting them, then they're not serving the client to the be st of their ability. They're going to forget what they were doing, might make a mistake, or forget to follow-up with something they're supposed to send to the client.

Team members need to schedule intentional intervals. If they go back and forth between unrelated activities, get interrupted and distracted, their client service will suffer.

Jen's Jots

- Schedule a specific time block each day for handling client service calls and needs.

- If a dient calls you when you're occupied with something else, slot a return call to them in a designated block, not a specific time.

- Don't try to provide seNice when you can't dedicate 100 percent of your time and attention to that seNice. Manage and schedule the time when you can offer 100 percent effort.

✳ Are You Playing Offense or Defense?

> **The Big Idea:** Use your day to play offense. Base your time-compressed schedule around prospecting for new business
>
> "'Complacency...When you're busy it's easy"
>
> -Anonymous

It's a cliche in football: defense wins championships. If you mostly play defense in your mortgage practice, however, all you'll win is a chance to try a different profession. You have to play offense.

Are you playing offense or defense in your practice? Do you spend your day *reacting* to what's happening, or do you spend your day making things happen and professionally responding?

Here's what playing *defense* feels like:
*   Reading emails.
*   Emailing people instead of picking up the phone.
*   Surfing the web.
*   Running errands.
*   Answering status update calls.
*   Clearing conditions.
*   Returning phone calls.
*   Clarifying terms and fees.
*   Solving problems/putting out fires.
*   Explaining the next steps in the process.
*

And, here's what playing *offense* feels like:

*   Communicate proactively with clients and partners on loan status updates.
*   Sales visits with past clients and referral partners.
*   Following up on leads.

- Making outbound phone calls.
- Socializing at networking events.
- Posting social media announcements.
- Hosting client and referral partner appreciation events.
- Marketing to your database for more referrals.
- Attending a closing.
- Teaching a class.
- Conducting a discovery meeting with a client.
- Uninterrupted time completing a loan analysis.

Spend more time on offense. This puts you in "scoring position" to provide Five Star service, resulting in more referrals and happier clients.

In a nutshell, playing offense is about positioning yourself as a leader who is proactive and who leans into their practice, instead of sitting back waiting for the next issue to present itself.

Every interaction (via email, phone, or in person) by you, your team, or a person at your company either deposits or withdraws from your client's trust account. A short, nasty email by an upset processor or your lack of control when being chal lenged about your rates all create withdrawals and moves clients and partners away from you and your practice.

But things such as a quick, comforting phone call to explain the need for more documents or a fast one-minute voicemail to a real estate agent to update them on the loan status so they can sell more homes instead of worrying about whether you are doing your job create huge deposits in the big picture and take no time at all.

This is the true difference between offense and defense. What does your daily plan and mindset look like?

- Do you come to work every day thinking about your transactions that are in process or falling apart? Well, that's where you'll focus your time and energy.

- Do you come to work focused on finding another client? Well, then you'll direct your energy and time doing exactly that!

- Do you put a priority on your emails, transaction issues, and conditions that need clearing? These are things that need attention. *Just don't think you always have to work on them first!*

How to Get on Offense

Anticipate. Anticipate. Anticipate. You can become an offensive professional by being proactive on all fronts. It's not that complicated!

Don't allow clients or real estate agents to call *you* for updates. Anticipate and reach out first. Get back to the basics:

♦ Call/email updates to all parties in a transaction, or to just chat.

♦ Schedule appointments for continued healthy relationships!

♦ Pick up the phone and call your referral partners. Ask for a coffee, lunch, or office appointment.

♦ Make your 1st and 10 calls.

♦ Pay attention and look for signs that someone needs more handholding, is confused about something, or is struggling to get you a document you requested.

♦ Put meetings on your calendar. If you have appointments on your calendar you'll keep them no matter how busy you think you are.

You're not even in the game if you are simply waiting for the next ball to drop so you can react rather than respond.

Get on the offense, talk to people , make contacts, and ask for opportunities. More of that business will come to you. There is plenty of business available for people who show true professionalism

Service Your Clients Offensively

If you get a call or email from a client or real estate agent asking you about the status of a loan, you just lost the game! You are now on the defense to updat e and explain the status. These calls are negativ e and time-consuming. They leave your clients wondering if they can trust or count on you; worse yet, they may feel you are not accountable and therefore they need to hover over you the rest of the way to closing for fear of you dropping the ball.

Offensive calls, on the other hand, create a positiv e response by all and put you in a position of strength. Anticipate your clients' needs and questions. Touch base frequently, even if just to say hello and check in on their emotional state through the process. Eve ry tim e you call and they see your name and numb er it will create a deposit in their trust account.

Use Your Time for Smart Action

By now, you know how much value I place on using time efficiently and smartly.

Using your time for smart action is a core strategy for advancing your mortgage practice by leaps and bounds:

◆ Discipline yourself to follow a plan for each day.

◆ Compress your work into time blocks and intentional intervals.

◆ Work with intensity and focus during those intervals.

◆ Play offense.

Jen's.Jots

◆ Think about where you've prioritized your time over the past week. Have you spent more time and focus on transactions than on prospecting?

◆ Think about how you can flip your priorities so you're spending most of your time playing offense-finding new business.

✴ Defining Your Role?

> **The Big Idea:** The Finder, Minder, and Grinder roles are all important to the successful operation of your mortgage practice. It is you, as the Finder, who drives the growth and success of the business.
>
> "If you want to be massively successful, get clean on why you're here.... with meaning, money and fulfillment!"
>
> - Jen Du Plessis

To utilize your time to the best of your ability, i.e.,working in your Genius Zone, you mustfirst identify the role(s) you will play. Let me ask you a serious question: What is the central, most important role you have in your practice? And here's the crucial follow-up question: Are you fulfilling thatrole?

In my experience, I've found that many loan officers haven't thought about those questions. And that's not good. If you don't really know what your first-and-fore most role is, you may spend a shortened career in mortgage lending, spinning your wheels,wasting crucial time, and never gaining the traction needed to reach your goals. Right now, in this year in our industry and these times of endless technological advancement, if you are standing still and doing nothing to advance your practice and life, you are moving backward, and very fast. If you live in, or know about, an area of the country that has horrible traffic, this example will be perfect. I live in the suburbs of Washington, D.C. (the District) and with that comes traffic! If I leave my home at 6:00 am, I am sure to make it to a meeting in the District on time at 8:00 am. But if I leave just 15 minutes later,I won't make it until 9:00 am maybe.

It's the same in your career-if youdon't leave now,you maynot make it in time.

In my thoughts and observations over my now 34-year career in lending, I've developed and implemented three principal roles that people have in mortgage lending. Each of the three is vital to the efficiency and timely operation of a mort gage practice (or any business for that matter), but only one of these roles sparks the growth and financial success of a practice.

The first role is that of being a Finder. The **Finder** is the person who generates and finds the business and develops the relationships that lead to referrals. This is the role I play on my team. I refer to myself as a Lead Generation Machine.

The second role is that of being the Minder. The **Minder** is the person who makes sure the loan transaction process runs smoothly and all parties involved can be kept up to date and communicated with. I call this person the Maestro.

The third role is that of being the Grinder. The **Grinder** is the person who orga nizes the day-to-day business tasks, such as database management, outgoing lead generating phone calls, creating and printing flyers, putting seminar and class packages together, tending to the Finder's schedule, event planning, expense reports and budgets, and more. This can either be one role or two. When your practice is large enough, this will be the latter. This is my Database Manager and my Marketing Director.

Now, some of you may be saying to yourself, "Gosh, I'm all three of those." And you may well be! But to be overwhelmingly successful in this industry, you can't be all three at one time. We all start at the same place, so it can be done, but my opinion is that it can't be done for any sustainable period of time if you want to close a lot of business.

To have a growth mindset, you need to focus most your time and effort on finding business. Your goal is to move the vast bulk of the *Minder* and *Grinder* roles onto your team. Note: I do not refer to any of my team members as "assistant," nor should you. No one wants to be handed-off to someone of perceived lesser value. Your team members are your partners, managers, and directors.

We'll have a look at what it means to have a *Finder* mindset, and we'll also take a deep dive into the daily things you must do to be a *Finder* and discuss the vital aspect of finding business through referral partners.

You can also view Finding, Minding, and Grinding as attitudes or ways of thinking. There are process-related, customer service business-building, and activities that you must conduct as a *Minder.* There are also basic maintenance activities in your business and life that you must pay attention to as the *Grinder.*

We'll look at each of these positions in the three sections that follow. You may also want to consider the requirement of each team member to read this book so they can be crystal clear on their role on your team.

I'm packing three decades of practical experience into the following sections; experience that has enabled me to reach the top of my profession.

Roles and Mindset

Defining your role as a *Finder* goes back to our discussion about developing a vision for your practice, formulating a business plan, and setting goals for what you want to achieve. It is easy to see how defining your role as the *Finder* will be the determining factor for success or failure in achieving your vision and goals.

I continually assess the highest and best use of my time in order to refine and sharpen my role as the *Finder* in my practice. That's something I hope you can also begin to do. Continually refining my role enables my team and me to be the most efficient we can be, AND it enables us to serve our clients at a very, very high level of satisfaction.

Finder

As the *Finder,* your sole role is to find, meet with, and develop strong business relationships with referral partners, clients, online lead aggregators, etc., who will provide leads or send referrals to your practice. It's also your job to conduct and attend seminars to gain momentum, expansion, and exposure for your practice; to hold client parties, business mixers, pop-bys to partner and client offices and homes; to network, structure loans, present options to clients; or anything that will put money on the table. Period.

Minder

The *Minder* is the person who makes sure that the loan process runs smoothly, who collects the documents from the borrower and reviews the documents. Your *Minder* should be a really good loan processor or underwriter who is tired of "talk ing to paper" and wants to talk to people. This can also be a loan officer who is great with guidelines on the phone, but for one reason or another has never really been able to bring in business.

The *Minder* is the person who is managing all the transaction activities because, quite frankly, you can't serve your clients properly by spreading yourself too thin. You can't be meeting with a customer for a discovery meeting, for example, while getting pinged by phone calls and emails from other borrowers. So the *Minder* needs to be the person who is scheduling appointments, who is managing your emails and responding quickly to requests by borrowers while you are building your business and bringing in more loans. They are the Operation Manager and Orchestra Conductor in your practice. There isn't beautiful music if someone isn't overseeing everything.

You might be in a position where you are a one person show, have just one assis tant helping you (and they are acting as both a *Minder* and *Grinder),* or the two of you are sharing the roles. Either way, if you have the capacity, please find another assistant immediately. An assistant will change your business dramatically. If you commit to consistent *Finder* activities you will need these people soon enough, I promise.

Grinder

The *Grinder* manage s your precious database first and foremost, either in an administrative function or in a sales role. This person, if functioning in both roles, spends the first part of their day in the sales role-making outgoing lead generat ing, nurturing, and retention phone calls to partners and clients-and then spends the latter half of the day with database entry and management, putting together your mailers, managing expenses, administrative duties, or handling marketing efforts for your team. Virtually everything they do supports the Finder's activities.

You can also consider a part-time assistant by adding someone to your team for a few hours a day. The person is not going to be involved with loan files, but can perform peripheral duties like putting packages together for classes and presen tations, or getting flyers produced, or posting for you on Facebook- just a ton of things really. Your time is worth much more than the $10 or $15 you'll have to pay a part-time person, so it will be worthwhile to shed those *Grinder* duties.

Jen's Jots

♦ Each of the three roles-Finder, Minder, and Grinder-is necessary for the successful operation of a mortgage practice. You can 't be all three and hope to do it for very long. However, with good time compr ession habits you will be able to enjoy the current production you have even by func tioning in all the roles.

♦ As the Finder, you must grow your practice by bringing in business and developing relationships that generate referrals and leads.

What is Your Role

♦ Finder (CEO)
  > Rainmaker
  > Gatekeeper
  > Business Development Officer

♦ Minder (COO)
  > Process/Operations
  > Transaction Flow
  > Customer Service

♦ Grind e r (CFO)
  > Database Management
  > Administrative Duties
  > Lead Generation, Nurturing & Retention

SECTION 4.
FINDER

✳ The Lead Generation Machine

> **The Big Idea:** To catapult your practice, you must develop and practice a Finder mindset and attitude and you must be a lead-generation machine. You must consistently initiate lead-generation activities
>
> "Each and every day, someone somewhere in the city needs my services, My job TODAY is to find that person."
>
> *- Michael J. Maher*

I believe this section is the most crucial part of this book because this is where you, as a Loan Officer, should reside, The most important aspect in your practice is developing new business. Nothing else matters when you haven't developed relationships and/or have new leads coming into your pipeline continuously.

You have made the decision to be in an industry that is inherently difficult and stressful. Sales is inherently rich with rejection, When you accept this,you can move on to the thought that, "Okay, I'm in this world, how can I make it a really valuable and rich life?" My recommendationis to choose the activities, products, and people that make you resonate and smile, and then run your business from there. If it's workings withveterans, do VA loans and then become the best.If it's working with single women, start there. Your business will grow and one starting point willlead to many others. The seeds will have then been planted for remark able growth. Start with one or two points of interest, of passion, and the business planthat you develop around this real solid core willunfold in avery gracious and authentic way, Thal will give you a sense of value in our industry and to those you connect with-attributes of a true Finder.

As the *Finder,* each of your priorities need to focus on lead-generating activi ties, or LGAs. You must get your lead-generating activities done first in your daily schedule. These are your daily phone calls, meeting and working with referral partners, meeting and talking with clients, and structuring loans. And there are a myriad other LGAs you should be thinking about and initialing,

I guess that's the key to being a *Finder* ... you always needto be initialing, reach ing out, extending yourself, and finding new ways lo pull partners and prospects into your orbit.

Initiating business comes first, before customer service, If your systems are rock solid,this should be a breeze for you. I certainly don't mean that you give second-rate customer service since your business growth depends completely on referrals and your reputation and customer experiences-of course you have to deliver top-shelf customer service. But in terms of your daily time priorities, finding comes first, customer service is second. When you add a Minder to your team, this dynamic will shift.

Where It All Comes Together

The ideas I share with you in this book are meant to converge into one result: making you a better *Finder*.

When I share about creating your vision and plan and formulating goals for your practice, all those thoughts are predicated on your ability to find prospects and bring in business and leads. When I talk about ideas for controlling your daily schedule and blocking your time to get more done, those ideas are all aimed at making you much more efficient in generating leads and business. When I discuss strategic relationships to attract and work with referral partners, those ideas are directed toward leveraging your connections to bring in more leads.

My hope is that I'd like you to think one thought as you read each page and chapter of this section, and really the entire book: How can I apply these ideas to becoming a better *Finder?*

Even better, what I really want you to do is think this every hour of every day: Is what I'm doing right now going to make me a better *Finder?* Is what I'm doing right now going to help me reach my goals and build my practice? If-and I hope it's not true-that your honest answer is "No," then I want you to step back and evaluate *why* you aren't becoming a better *Finder* and reaching your business goals. At the end of the day, you have to be able to look back and answer "Yes" to these questions:

♦ Am I engaging?

♦ Am I leaning in?

♦ Am I passionate?

♦ Am I growing professionally?

♦ Am I creating richer relationships?

♦ Am I leaning into my business?

♦ Am I being true to myself? Authentic?

♦ Am I making every minute count?

♦ Am I curious?

♦ Am I making every day count?

As a *Finder,* you should make the most of your time. What I'm suggesting is you put on the blinders and focus on things that are important in your practice to move the needle. First do the things that are important to bring in more business, do them well, and do them in the most efficient way you possibly can. Always challenge yourself to improve how you go about finding new business, new prospects, and new leads.

Recognize and Embrace Your Role

In order to build your practice, you need to know exactly what your role is and *not deviate from that role* for even one day.

If there is one-honestly there are way too many-thing I've learned it's that there is so much you need to do in a day and it's crucial to be able to fashion the best time to do the most important aspects that lead to new business. And please, always focus on business-building activities from 9 to 5. That is not the time to be working on your budget or printing flyers for next week. Do that later if you have to do it yourself.

During the business day, build blocks of time exclusively for business building, for lead generation, for meeting with referral partners, and for moving your practice forward. Recognize what your most important role is and then block your time to accomplish that role. Make sure you put those pieces into your daily calendar.

One rule of thumb to start with is to consider prospecting a minimum of 20 hours per week, keeping in mind that prospecting isn't necessarily just making phone calls, but it's also being in front of people. The first thing you might do in the morning is make your phone calls from 9 to 10, then holding your weekly profit partner calls, then conducting two face-to-face meetings. You might meet with a real estate agent, a client for a discovery meeting, another type of referral partner, or attend a networking lunch. These are all lead-generating activities.

In the book *Never Eat Alone,* which talks about reaching out to your circle of contacts all the time, one message is exactly what the title commands: don't eat alone. Use mealtime to meet with a client, to take a past client to lunch, to have breakfast. So if you're making calls in the morning say from 9 to 10, and then you have an appointment at 10, lunch with somebody, and then you have an appointment at 2, right there you have done lead-generating activities as the *Finder* for most of the day.

But if that's what you're doing as the *Finder* and you are also the *Minder,* now you're stressed. If you've been accomplishing *Finder* activities for nearly the entire day, when are you going to find time to follow up with all the referrals? When are you going to get to following up with paystubs and W2s and loan analysis on a client? If that's the situation you find yourself in, it doesn't make sense that you don't have help. Even if it's just you and a loan officer assistantand you're sharing the *Grinding* duties, it just doesn't make sense to try to go it alone. You are holding yourself back. I beg you, please get out of your own way, embrace fully your role as a *Finder,* delegate much of the rest of your practice to a *Minder* assistant, and then you can move forward and succeed.

If you can't, don't, or won't get an assistant then here's your crash course on carrying both roles. Make phone calls every day. Meet people two days a week (Tuesday and Thursday) but hold four appointments each day so you can *Mind* and *Grind* on the opposing days.

Finder Basics: People, Time, Activities

I encourage you to tackle the basics, the people, time, and activities that generate leads. Stop wasting money, time, and effort on shiny objects and the next big thing in technology for marketing. Finding more business boils down to tackling the basics and doing that consistently day after day:

♦ Use the phone. A *Finder* initiates contact with partners and clients. Make the calls you should make, not just the calls you have to make. Daily phone calls create and sustain momentum.

♦ Meet people face to face. It makes your relationships stronger, and it gives you the opportunity to dig deeper into how you can help each other.

♦ Send thank-you notes to everyone for anything and everything. If you're making 10 daily calls, meeting with partners, meeting with prospective partners, conducting a seminar, and doing all the other lead generation activities you should be doing as a *Finder,* you should be sending out 70 to 80 (or more!) thank-you cards a week.

♦ Continually cultivate and work with referral partners. Form relationships with a wide variety of professional partners, from real estate agents, to financial planners, to divorce attorneys, to title company owners, and on and on. They will be a goldmine of business.

♦ Build and maintain your contact community database. This will quickly become the heart of your practice and may eventually account for *most* of your annual business.

♦ Differentiate yourself. Find ways to separate yourself from other lenders and come up with new, fresh ideas to generate new business. You're expected to have good rates. You're expected to close on time. You're expected to have good customer service. You need to find ways to go beyond all those basics and differentiate yourself in the market. Focus on WIIFM-What's In It *From* Me.

Your chances of success increase in proportion to the number of times you reach out to partners and clients. That is why I engage in so many communication activities-to keep me top of mind with all my prospects and create richer relationships for all.

Raise your *Finder* skills to new levels. Take one idea and implement it with vigi lance to create a strong new habit. Then initiate the next idea, action, or system you would to incorporate into your practice. Whatever you do will work for you IF you do it consistently. This is the key to generating new leads and prospects day after day, week after week, month after month. Focused, consistent work!

Jen's Jots

♦ Embrace and define your role as the *Finder* for your practice. Your poten tial success lies with your ability to bring in business.

♦ Focus first on the basics: the people, time, and activities that will generate leads for your practice.

♦ Work on business-building activities first.

♦ Don't try to do it alone. Hire a person or people to be your *Minders* and

♦ *Grinders* so you can do the most important thing: bring in business.

✳ The Buying Window

> **The Big Idea:** *Keepin touch with clients over the long term, so you can stay top of mind when they enter the buying window.*
>
> *"Know where your salesincreases will come from.*
> *They won't just happen."*
>
> *- Byrd Baggett*

Let me ask you a quick question. How many of you have contacted a client or friend, only to find out they just bought a new home or refinanced their current loan and you didn't even know they were in the market to make a move? What happened? Well,somehow you missed their *buying window.*

The buying window is the time frame during which someone's <u>desire</u> to purchase a new or different home meets with their perfect <u>timing</u> to begin taking action.

You must ensure they think of you when they're in their buying window. This is important for generating repeat business from clients for the annuity income of your practice,

Your challenge will always be how to keep yourself top of mind so that clients reach out to you when theyfirst enter the buying window, Of course, that's easier said than done! You don't know EXACTLY when they're going to enter the buying window phase.

To give you the best chance of catching them in their buying window is to move beyond the basics when you call a client. Use the opportunity to assess whether they're entering the buying window. Ask questions.

Whenever you make a call to a past client, it's important to dig deeper than the standard scripts we discussed in the last few chapters, such as "Hi,it's Jen, I'm just checking in on you," That may not be extensive enough. You may want to ask them things resembling, "Do you still like the house?", "Any new family mem bers?", or similar open-ended questions, You want to determine through intelligent questioning and active listening for clues as to whether they're getting close to another buying window or perhaps a refinancing window. Of course, buying win dows are frequently revealed during interest rate drops and when conduction annual mortgage reviews, These suggested scripts are in addition so you don't miss one single opportunity,

The only way to ensure success in this is to be in front of clients as frequently as possible; via email, phone calls,visiting with them one-to-one, doing their annual mortgage review,whatever the reason to stay top-of-mind. Please recognize that sometimes your efforts may not be enough. When they do get into the buying window and they haven't talked to you for several months or since the last time you did an annual review, someone else may get the loan. It is just how it works.

When you think about all the loans you've done over your career, compared to the number of people who have called you out of the blue some years later,the numbers don't compare. I had a clientwho I had worked with10years ago call me out of the blue for a new loan. I had been in touch with her all that time, but I didn't know she was looking to buy, and worse, I'll admit,I didn't know she had gotten married. That created a buying window. Luckily, she loved me enough that she called, but boy, I can count on one hand when those situations have happened. It's different when you know there's a buying window.

Keep in touch with your clients as frequently as possible, and when you are in touch make sure that you're asking the right questions to dig a little deeper and chat about life events that are happening. Their answers will give you clues that a buying window may be opening up.

Jen'sJots

♦ Keep in touch with clients as frequently as possible, and when you are in touch ask questions that dig deeper into their life events.

♦ Asking the right questions may reveal they are entering a buying window andyou'll be in a position to generate repeat business and help your client again.

✳ Action Mindset

The Big Idea: *Always follow the three-part strategy of the Trifecta of Success to determine exactly which activities you should be doing.*

"What keeps you extraordinary vs ULTRA extraordinary?"
-Anonymous

One way that you can zero in on core action to drive your business is to use something I call the Trifecta of Success. I also refer to it as the Trinity of Triumph, because I'm Catholic, so I always use references related to my faith. I've also heard this referred to as the hedgehog method.

The first part of this three-pronged strategy is to **only takeaetion on ordo things that you areabso/utelyex.eelkntatdoing.** So if you aren't good on the phone because thatmakes you feel uncomfortable and you're better at talking to some one in person, then only do activities thatyou can do in person, such as network
ing, speaking to groups, having small workshops, or book clubs. If you're better at being on the phone and don't like networking events, then hire someone to be your business development officer who goes to those events on your behalf. I've seen that work very well with a chiropractor, so I don't want you to be afraid of doing something like that for mortgage lending. A chiropractor in my BNI group had a business development officer who came in and talked about the chiroprac tor.

You want to act as if you're the doctor in a medical practice. You don't want to be the receptionist, and the nurse, and the doctor, and the billing and collections people all rolled into one. You want to be the expert. Don't be afraid to do certain things that you are trying to master.just set it up so that it works for you in your market.

Again, you want to do those things that you're absolutely excellent at doing. If you aren't good at it, hire someone else who is. And hire someone else whose strength is your weakness, don't hire someone else who isn't good at it either. That's not going to get you anywhere.

Second, *only do what youabsolutely Jove* to *do.* If you don't like networking, don't do it. If you don't like reviewing tax returns, then by all means, stop doing it.

Third,*only do what makes money sense.* Does spending $500 a month to co-brand yourself with a real estate agent on Zillow make money sense for your prac tice? Does sponsoring a broker open that costsyou $100 for food-plus $100 or
$150 for a gift certificate prize that's used by a real estate agent who you'll never see again and most likely won't want to meet you later-make money sense for your practice? Of course, I'm discussing things that don't make money sense for my practice. You have to make that decision for your practice.

There are so many shiny objects that we see. We hear what other people are doing all the time and we want to jump on the bandwagon. But many things just really might not make money sense for you.

I'll give you a good example. I partner with a real estate agent who I really like; she's fairly new in the business and she is in-and-out with giving me referrals. She's not one of my strategic partners, but she's someone I like. She called me out of the blue and asked me if I could join her on a conference call where some one was going to try to sell us, for $799 a month, an Internet lead site. For me, that's not even close to the type of business I want to do. It was a very easy deci sionto say no.

I'm not interested in spending money for Internet-generated leads. I'm not good at working with rate-shopper phone calls, and you know what,I don't like doing it either. I don't want to be a commodity. Now if your practice does lead generat ing from the Internet, then absolutely do it as long as it meets the criteria of the Trifecta of Success.

Let me get back to the three components of the Trifecta:
♦ Only do what you are really, really good at.
♦ Only do what you really, really love to do.
♦ And only do what makes money sense.

Note that I didn't say what makes money, but what makes money sense. There's a real key difference here.I strongly encourage you that if there is something that makes money sense, and it's something you really love to do, and you're just not quite good enough at it, then improve your skills. If two of the points on this tri angle are strong, and the third area can make sense for you down the road if you do a few things differently or tweak a few things, then by all means pursue it. But keep track of the results and give yourself a deadline where you'll stop doing the activity if it's not coming together. If two or all three of these points on the triangle aren't working for you,sayno!

I'm going to give you a good example, and this is the example I give to everybody. I'm excellent at analyzing tax returns.I'm really good because I was an underwriter and it's one of my strengths. People bring in piles of tax returns and ask me to analyze them. The thing is, I don't like doing it anymore. I used to, but not these days. And,oh,bythe way, it does not make money sense for me to be sitting and reviewing tax returns for 20 or 30 minutes when I could be making another five phone calls or I could be having a quick coffee with one of my strategic partners. So for me, when considering whether I should review tax returns, only one of the three points works for me. I am really good at reviewing tax returns, but I do not like to do it and it does not make money sense for me. Does that make sense?

Therefore, I don't review tax returns anymore. Instead, my production partner reviews them because she loves doing it, she is excellent at it, and it makes money sense for my practice to have her do the review rather than me.

So every time someone asks you to do something, whether it's "Canyou meet me for coffee?", 'Will you go with me to a networking event?", "Can you take a look atthis file?",or 'Will yousponsor this open house or this event?",please stop and ask yourself these three questions.

That is the essence of taking smart action.

Jen's Jots

♦ To make the highest and best use of your time, always ask yourself:

♦ Is this something I'm really,really good at?

♦ Is this something I really, really love to do?

♦ Does it make money sense for me to do this?

✳ Let Go to Climb Higher

The Big Idea: The growth of your practice and income begins when you let go of things you do now that don't directly contribute to business growth.

"You can do more with what you already have than what you are currently doing."

-Anonymous

Can you devote more time and energy to being a *Finder* while still doing every thing you do now? In other words, can you prospect more, find more business, and double or eventriple your income if you hold onto all the other daily activities involved in your practice?

You and I can agree that will most certainly not happen.

We've all heard about climbing the ladder of success. What I want to share with you is an analogy about the ladder of success that I think will really help you in thinking about being a stronger *Finder*.

While coaching, I've had several conversations with loan officers who really resist changing the way they do business. What they say is they want to do more busi ness but they aren't willing to let go of certain things they're doing now. I know that if you don't have an assistant or you don't feel totally comfortable moving a large share of the processing responsibilities to your assistant, this may be an area you struggle with. You don't want to let go of the fact that you've handled everything and that you feel you can or should continue to handle everything. Do you often think, "They want me, they don't want my assistant."

Or maybe you're what I call a helicopter loan officer. You hover over everybody during the loan process because you're so fearful that the loan isn't going to go right unless you're intimately involved in every step, so you covet and hold onto the file.

The bad news is this behavior is preventing you from reaching higher and higher levels of business and income. At some point you have to give up some of the things that made you successful and pass them along to someone else to handle for you.

Do you think Microsoft would be the mega-company it is today if Bill Gates never gave up doing the things he did when he started the company? He started Microsoft in his garage with a card table for a desk. He did everything. He went out and got the business. He managed the business. He was grinding out work and doing research. Doing the books. Writing the programs. He did everything. Can you imagine if he never let go of doing all of that and decided that he was the only one who could do all those things, and that the only way for him to grow was to work harder and put in longer hours? But he did let go of doing the things that he wasn't good at and he let other people do those things.

Climbing the Ladder of Success

So it's the same thing with you. Picture a ladder. The two vertical parts of a ladder are called rails and the horizontal steps are called rungs. Let's imagine that each rung on the ladder represents $500,000 a month in closings.

In order to go to the next rung on a ladder, you have to let go of the previous rung. That's how you climb up. If you're doing $500,000 a month in production and you want to get to a million dollars a month, you're going to have to let go of something that you're doing at the $500,000 level so you can get to the million dollar level.

So think about where you are on this ladder of success and then think about how you are going to get to the next level.

To climb up the ladder you must find more business. You either have to devote more time to developing new business, work on developing new and more prom ising partnerships, or both. To accomplish a higher level of *Finding,* you will have to give up something else that you're doing on a lower rung.

Should you let go of gathering documentation and let someone else do that? Should you let go of managing the entire file yourself? Maybe you should let go of some partners who have fallen off and develop partnerships with new referral partners. Maybe you are working with real estate agents who were new to the business four years ago and are still low-producing agents who you're holding onto. Do you think you need to let go of partners that you're clinging to but aren't coming through for you? The people who got you to your current success may not be the people who will get you to your next level.

Maybe you're not delegating enough to allow yourself to get to the next level. Maybe you're not making enough phone calls and you need to get past the fear of making phone calls, or the fear of making sales calls, or the fear of calling a real estate agent or a referral partner and asking to meet for coffee so you can determine if they're a good quality fit for you.

Maybe you need to let go of doing a certain type of product. This is not to criticize anyone who's doing a certain type of product, but if you're soliciting USDA loans then that's the kind of loan you're going to get. They typically are lower loan amounts, they are more complex, and as a result, that might be holding you back from getting more business and other types of loans.

Think about what you're projecting to the world as your niche and what you can let go of. Maybe you need to let go of doing *less* lucrative loans and pass those on to someone else in your office who is lower on the rung and needs more busi ness. This will free you up to do *more* lucrative loans to continue your climb on the ladder of success.

Think about it. What can you let go to go higher? What can you let go of to be able to do more business? How can you move to the next level?

Learning to Let Go
Loan officers become successful not just by what they're doing now but by what they learn to let go of. I can tell you from my perspective, with my volume, I've let go of a lot of things-a tremendous amount of things. For example, I don 't write my own thank-you notes anymore. You wouldn't know I don't write the notes because I finally reached a level of trust with my team member who is writing them after they have learned my style.

I had to let go of running AUS myself. I can just review the findings if I want, but quite frankly I had to let go of that. I trust that my team is looking at the findings and analyzing the loan thoroughly and that they will alert me to anything of con cern.

I had to stop participating in every pipeline meeting. It's more important for me to be debriefed on the meeting highlights. It can include both small and large tasks and activities. Free yourself to do the things that you do very well. Think of this as building muscle as you're going up those many rungs, building your muscles and your skills in the areas that enable you to go higher and higher. Remember that every successful loan officer did not become successful just by doing what they're doing now. They became successful because they learned to let go.

Here's the question: What do you need to let go of? What are the things that you need to let go of so you can climb the ladder of success? The sooner you do it, the faster you're going to get there.

Jen's Jots

♦ Let's get moving up! Identify the activities, products, tasks, or partner s you can let go of so you can move up to more lucrative activities, products, or partners.

♦ Become more successful not just by what you're doing now,but by learn ing to let go so you can do the most important thing-bring in more busi ness.

✳ Lean into Your Practice

The Big Idea: *Play on offense, not defense, so you can lean into your practice and find more business. You simply can't wait for business to come to you.*

"My suggestion would be to walk away from the 90% who don't... and join the 10% who do."

-Jim Rohn

Being a *Finder* is all about leaning into your business. Being a *Finder* means you initiate business-building and lead-generating activities every day. What it really comes down to is that you play offense, not defense, in your practice.

There are thousands of people buying homes and refinancing loans every day. If you are stuck on defense, these customers will go to someone else. If you're on offense every day-talking to people, making contacts, asking for opportuni ties-more of the business will come to you.

Lean into your practice so you're *in* demand and not *on* demand.

When you're on defense, you're waiting for business and problems to come to you. You check your email, surf the web, or spend valuable time solving transac tion issues. You're waiting for something to happen so you can respond instead of proactively doing what is truly important.

When you're on offense and leaning into your business, you're presenting your self in a positive and proactive light. You're meeting face-to-face with referral part ners, you're making your daily 1st and 10 phone calls, you're networking, you're hosting seminars, you're communicating with clients, and you're holding apprecia tion events. You're initiating the plays and dictating the action.

It's not that hard to switch your style of work from defense to offense. There are a handful of core actions you can take to put yourself in "scoring position" to find another customer and write another loan.

Here's my 5-part game plan for leaning into your business:

Sell First, Service Second

You'll grow your practice when you sell first and service second. If you come to work every day thinking about your transactions in process, that's where you'll focus your time and energy. If you come to work focused on finding another prospect, you'll direct that same energy into doing just that.

Now, I'm not telling you to ignore your transaction issues and the administrative details in your practice, just don't think you always have to tackle these things first. Better yet, let others on your team tackle issues around loans for you.

Join Organizations

Get involved in business and professional groups. Join a networking club, a business circle, or a community group. This will get you out of the office and on the offense. You'll get away from your computer and email, and you'll get in front of more people, more prospects, and more opportunities.

Learn to Sell

If you've transitioned in the industry through the underwriting or transaction processing side of things, you may not have the sales skills you need to bring in prospects and loans. The good news is you can learn to sell. There are resources everyvvhere that you can tap into.

Hire a coach, go to sales training workshops, or read good books on selling and subscribe to sales-themed magazines and online publications. You can develop the sales skills you need to spark your practice.

Get Out of the Office

Nothing beats meeting people face-to-face for generating leads. Set appointments, because once you set them you'll keep them. Pick up the phone and call your referral partners and ask to meet them for a coffee, lunch, or office appointment.

Hoping you can get out every week and see people is a poor offensive strategy. It's just not going to happen. If you have appointments set, you'll keep them no matter how busy you think you are.

Get Organized

If you're disorganized, you'll spend a lot of time on defense. Put systems in place for everything you do and use the technology and utilities available to you to manage transactions and client communications. Start using the time management technique of time compression to get more done in less time.

Lean Forward

Defense is about reacting to what's happening. Offense is about anticipating, responding proactively, and making things happen. Sure, it's easier to live life on defense. It seems safer, and you don't have to put yourself out there, but you're always on your heels, never leaning forward on your toes.

Lean forward, lean into your business. The more you lean forward, the faster your practice will grow and the more your income will grow.

Jen's Jots

♦ As a *Finder* you must make things happen, not wait for them to happen.

♦ Lean into your business so you 're always generating new opportunities for growth.

✳ Time Block Your Way to Growth

> **The Big Idea:** Get more done and find more business by using time blocking / time compression as a way to keep yourself focused completely on one type of task for a defined period of time.
>
> "Each day you get better or worse. It's your choice."
>
> - Byrd Baggett

Your daily mission as a *Finder* should be focused overwhelmingly on one thing: Bringing in new leads and business into your practice. We've already established how important that is compared to anything else you do.

Since prospecting is the most important thing you do in your practice, you really must follow a daily schedule that is centered on looking for business. That is how you set yourself up for success: by making sure you are consistently doing your most important activities.

Whatever you want to call it-time blocking or time compression-this practice has been critical to my success. Over the years I would never have been able to do the volume that I've done in my career if I hadn't used time blocking and time compression.

What is time blocking or time compression, really? Well, it's simply a mechanism for keeping yourself focused on one type of task for a set period of time. You schedule an hour or two, or whatever you feel is appropriate, to working on one thing and ONLY one thing-be it 1st and 10 phone calls, partner meetings, transaction management, a project,or business planning.

I hate to use the expression that you *force* yourself to work on only one thing, but that may be what you have to do. You *compel* yourself to give 100 percent of your attention to one type of task, one area of your practice, and one area *only* during the time you have scheduled for that activity. It's a jam session,a power hour. No interruptions,no calls,no email!

Why is this so important? There is so much thatyou need to do in a day. You need to carve out WHEN you should be doing the finding job and when you should be doing everything else.

Think about your work style. You go into the office and right away your time is chopped up into little, disconnected segments. You may get distracted by the bumblebee syndrome, buzzing from one thing to another. You let things pull you in, like the person who says, "Do you have a quick minute?" Or whenever your phone rings you actually answer it instead of waiting and calling people back, all at one time, after listening to your messages, all at one time.

Would you perform an everyday chore at home in little, chopped-up segments? Think about how you empty the dryer when you do the laundry. You take every thing out of the dryer all at the same time, right? You fold or hang everything up, all at one time, and place everything in like piles ... all the shirts, all the towels, all the socks, everything goes into a pile of like items or together according to their final destination. Then you walk those items together to the proper drawer or closet. Why do you do the laundry that way? Because it's more efficient!

Would it make any sense to grab one shirt, hang it on a hanger, walk it all the way to a bedroom, put this one shirt in the close\, then walk all the way back to the dryer,take out a towel,foldthe towel,walk it all the way to the bathroom, put the towel in the linen closet, then come all the way back to the dryer? And keep repeating that for every item in the dryer?

It seems ridiculous to think about doing laundry that way. The fact of the matter is that this is how most people work on a daily basis. They are so segmented, and they are one-and-done \askers or distracted mul\i\askers or task switchers. If you're a task switcher, you're constantly changing from task to task and you never get anything really deeply done. And when you do get it done, it might not be the best work that you probably could have done because you're trying to rush through it. So imagine again the dryer scenario where you are running back and forth between the dryer and some room with one item of clothing at a time and then coming backfor just one more item of clothing.

That's exactly what happens at work for most people. Eliminate that kind of work style by sticking to a time compressed or time blocked schedule.

Getting Started

Make it your goal to follow a time-compressed/ time-blocked schedule all day, every day. If your core work hours are 9:00 a.m. to 5:00 p.m., then I am a firm believer that all of that time should be scheduled in blocks (with appropriate "white space" between blocks for transitioning,traveling to a meeting, setting up a presentation, getting to a closing, getting a handful of one-minute tasks done, etc.).

See the sample weekly \ime-bloeked schedule I've included. This is how I actually schedule my week when I first began using time blocking.

Monday	Activity
6:30–7:30	Workout & Daily Affirmations
7:45–8:00	Organization of Day Review schedule, mapping, collateral, etc.
8:30–9:00	1st & 10s to A+/A Partners & Clients
10:00–11:00	1:1s or Client Meetings
Noon–1:00	Lunch with A+/A or Networking Meeting
2:00–3:00	1:1s or Client Meetings
3:00–5:00	Customer Service (Follow up, analysis, etc.)
6:00–6:30	Daily Reflection

Now, I don't expect you to go from zero to 60 in one day. Start by blocking your most important activities, and then stick to those blocks no matter what. After it becomes a solid habit, add another block of time.

The place to start, as I said, is to carve out when you should be doing your most important *Finding* activities: talking to and meeting with people in order to generate new business. Build blocks of time exclusively for business building, for lead generation, for daily phone calls, for meeting with referral partners, and for anything that moves your practice forward in terms of getting new business.

Perhaps you can start by setting an hour every day for making your 1st and 10 phone calls. Then add a two- or three-hour period once a week for meeting with referral partners. After that, block in specific times for client meetings throughout the week.

The crucial thing, though, is during those blocks don't allow yourself to be pulled from one task to another. Don't let your time be dictated by emails, phone calls, processing interruptions, and putting out fires in the office. Start by blocking time specifically dedicated to lead generating activities and you will virtually guarantee your success.

The Secret to Why Time Compression Works

The secret to why this practice will work for you is because you're working on just one task or type of task with a laser focus. Since you're totally focused you get the tasks completed in a shorter period of time than you would otherwise. Thus, you get more done, get it done well, and spend less time doing it. Win, win, win!

I call this working in intentional intervals. It means intentionally working during a period of time where you're 100 percent focused and dedicated to the task. You're dedicating 100 percent of your time and energy, versus maybe 50 percent of your effort to kind of doing something with an okay result.

When people think about using time blocking or time intervals, they think that doing so will restrict them, when actually it will do the opposite. It's going to pro vide you with *more* time and freedom. You will be much more efficient because you will be doing like-minded activities at the same time.

If I'm going to price a mortgage loan, why would I log in, price a loan, log out, answer a call, let someone interrupt me, and then have to price another loan so I have to go back in and log back in again? Why wouldn't I just go in and price all the loans at one time? It's much more efficient, like folding clothes all at once. Right? I promise, if you apply this efficiency to all your *Finder* activities, you will see your business take off.

Jen's Jots

♦   Make the most efficient use of your *Finding* time by following a time blocked or time compressed schedule.

♦   Start by carving out when you should be doing your most important activities: lead generation and finding new business.

♦   Work at 100 percent effort on one activity-work intentionally-during every time block of your day.

✳ 1st and 10-Do itAgain!

> **The Big Idea**: Every day, make phone calls to 10 of your past clients, prospects, credit clients, referral partners, real estate agents, and other members of your contact community to keep yourself top of mind, ask for referrals, and seek out new connections,
>
> 'Your chances of success increase in proportion to the number of sales calls you make."
>
> -Anonymous

If I had to pin down the handful of things that has made my mortgage practice successful, I'd start the list with my daily "1st and 10" phone calls. Making these calls has been one of the most powerful and impactful ways that I've advanced my practice over the years. They have made such a difference for me and they can make a huge difference for you.

Let's go over the fundamentals aboutthese calls.

The basic premise is that you make these daily Lead Generating Activity (LGA) calls during a time-blocked hour, calling people you *should* call and not to people you *need to call.* Carve out time for the need-to-call people in your daily schedule during your Transaction Management block.

On my team, every morning from 9:00 a.m. to 10:00 a.m. my team members and I are on the phone. We each make ten phone calls first thing in the morning. The difference is that the people that you *need to call* include perhaps a client that you're calling back to run through mortgage options with, a client to follow up on a paystub,or your processor to determine the status of an appraisal. Don't worry, you will get to these calls, but first things first! The *should call* individuals are past clients,prospects, partners, annual reviews, birthdays, anyone to simply say "hello" to; they definitely are not calls surrounding loans in process.

Listen,1" & 10s will generate leads and connections. These are positive,outgoing phone calls thatwill create greatness in your day.

Now,you may not have ten people to call, but down the road you will have ten people to call every day. I bet,though,you could find ten for today. What I'd like you to think about is this: Who is a prospect you received in the last week? That might be someone to call. Who did you close a loan with last month? Could you call that client? Who was the referral partner from that client? Who was the listing agent from that client? Or how about the title company for that particular client? Right there you have four people to call. But what about the person that you closed three months ago? Or a year ago? Or the prospect thatyou haven't talked to in six weeks? Or the new real estate agent that you'd like to have a meeting with? Or the new real estate agent that you met last night at a networking event? You can call people to mark occasions such as birthdays and anniversaries.

1st and 10s of Glance

What They Are:1st and 10 phone calls are daily lead generation calls to people you *should* call and not to people you *have* to call. You make these calls during a time you have blocked out every day on your calendar, ideally the first hour of your workday.

Who to Call: These calls are to 10 of your past clients, prospects, credit clients, referral partners, realtors, and service providers. I call these **"1st & 10s,"**then do it again tomorrow! Referral partners are anyone who provides a service to you or
who can or does provide you referrals or connections. This can range from an attorney to a hair dresser.

Whatto Say: You are simply checking in on them to see how they are doing and/or how their "season" was. What do I mean by "season?" Well, if we just passed a holiday, you can ask how was their Fourth of July or New Year. If there is no specific holiday that just happened, then ask how their summer, fall, spring, winter has been or if they had a goodweekend.

Why You're Calling: In addition to simply checking in because you care about them,you should have a purpose for the call just in case they ask,right? This is where you could be offering to bring them up to date with what is going on with rates, home sales, trends, new programs/products (and if they aren't interested I'll bettheyknow someone else who they canrefer!), or a personal invitation to a seminar or client appreciation event.

When to Ask for Business: At the end of the call thank them for their time and remind them that you have a vast network of home and financial service provid ers should they ever need a referral to someone AND that you appreciate them keeping you top of mind as well. It's just that easy! The conversion should be no more than five minutes, unless they have specific questions or needs.

OneMoreThing: This is where you put into practice your one-last-questiontech nique to get connections to more partners. "Oh,before we hang up. I'm always on the look-out for a great[fil in the blank]. Who do you know who is a great (fillin the blank]? If you do know someone, I'd appreciate an introduction."

What You've Just Done: In ten brief, five-minute phone calls you've kept yourself top of mind with ten members of your contact community, you've perhaps pro vided them some useful information, you've reminded them you love referrals, and you've possibly gotten a connection to even more partners. Now imagine what happens to your practice when you do this five days a week!

An Hour on Offense Protects Your Time

Now one of the things I've already mentioned is that I'm really an advocate of making sure that my time is kept precious. I'm very tightfisted about my time and I work hard to protect it.

Something I've found is that a lot of loan officers in our industry spend an exor bitant amount of time handling what I call defensive calls. I've already addressed this in Chapter 3-5.

Your 1st and 10 calls are positive and an offensive move. They should be a very short phone call, and the goal is to leave a good impact and impression on the person that you're calling. Plus, bonus, if you compact these ten calls into the first hour of your day, you've made the most of that precious hour of lead generation.

NOTE: As soon as I'm done with the calls I do an audio debrief for those with whom I had a conversation. You may be more comfortable making notes and then adding these notes to your contact database. To save yourself more time, write each person's name on a thank-you card envelope. Later in the day-say when you have a *Grinder* block of time-write all the thank-you notes for the day. Group them at the end of your day because throughout the day you may get referrals, have meetings, or sponsor a seminar. Just do them all at one time and knock them out. Boom, boom, boom!

What Do I Say? How Do I Start the Conversation?

While coaching and consulting, two questions always come up when I talk about 1st and 10s. The first is "Do I re ally hav e to make my daily phone calls, my 1st and 10s?" And the answer is: Yes, absolutely! The second question is, "Well, what do I talk about? How do I start th e co nve rsation?"

Repeat this mantra: "the season is the reason." Anytime you pick up the phone you can ask the client, the referral partner, the past client, "Hey, I'm just check ing in. How was your 'season'?" (What I really mean by this is, how was your weekend? How was your Fourth of July? How was your summer? How was your holiday?)

So again, "Hi, I'm just checking in, how was your 'season'?" Let them answer and respo nd accordingly. The next comment or question you can ask can be about content that is informative and provides value to them. Or it can simply be the following: "Well, listen, another reason for my call was just to let you know that I was thinking about you, and to remind you that I have an extensive network of home services and financial services so that if there's anything that you ever need, please don't hesitate to give me a call first, and I will make sure that my referral provides you with red carpet service."

Then you can briefly go into a substantive conversation tailored to that person's situation, perhaps talking about trends in the market, or inviting them to an upcoming seminar, or talking about new products you may be offering. At that point you can also remind them you always appreciate referrals.

And don't forget to ask that one last question that helps you expand your network! "Say, before we hang up, I'm always looking to meet a [fill in the blank-realtor, hair dresser, CFP, etc.] to better serve my clients. Who do you know who you would feel comfortable introducing me to?" That's a magic way to expand your prospect and referral partner connections.

It Gets Easier

The reason most Loan Officers don't make phone calls is because they don't want to seem "salesy" or don't feel they have a strong relationship with the person they are contacting. You may have had a great relationship with a client or partner throughout the entire purchase and loan process, everything was wonderful at closing, and you even received a great Zillow review. You had every intention of calling them, but you didn't. Now, over time, it's harder to make that phone call.

The more you communicate, the easier it is to pick up the phone. It becomes more difficult when you start stretching out the time between phone calls. So I just want to encourage you, please make those phone calls every day. Pick up the phone more consistently and it will become easier and easier to do. It may be that the first few times you try to do 1st and 10s you get cold feet or you overthink it. Then you end up not making the calls. It is so critical that you keep those relationships going with past clients and referral partners. Here's an idea. Make your first call to someone you like and have no problem calling. This will build your confidence so the next call is easier to make.

Jen's Jots

♦ Block out a time every day to make calls you SHOULD make to past cli ents, referral partners, and service partners.

♦ Make 10 of these calls the first thing in the morning-these are your 1st and 10s.

♦ These calls put you on the offense for finding business and generating leads, which is THE most important thing you must be doing to grow your practice.

✳ 3-2-1 Go!

> **The Big Idea:** If you can't get started with ten 1st & 10 calls every day for whatever reason, just do something to start reaching out to people you SHOULD call. Here's a way to ease into this vital daily task.
>
> *"Do not wait until the conditions are perfect to begin. Beginning makes the conditions perfect."*
>
> -Alan Cohen

Ten calls every day! How?

That's what I heard you say as you read the previous chapter. Ten calls can seem like a tall order, especially if you're relatively new to the mortgage industry or you haven't yet built up avery big o:>ntact community. You might be saying to yourself: "Jen,I can't possibly call 10 people a day! I don't have very many contacts on my database. If I call ten people a day, every day,I'll beback at the beginning of my listin a few weeks!"

If these calls are something you've not done before,you might find it a little chal lenging, a little overwhelming, to start calling 10 people per day, right out of the gate.

Not to worry. Making calls is about action and implementation, not necessarily about numbers. It's about consistently doing something every day to get more referrals, more connections, and more leads for your mortgage practice.

So here's an idea. I want to make this as easy as possible for you, but still ensure you make daily contact, so let's call this plan 3-2-1 Go.

Start by making *three* phone calls every morning to people that you should call. Let's say one is a real estate agent, one of your good partners and you call just to check in; next is a past client; and the third is either another referral source or a prospective client. Make three phone calls every day first thing in the morning. If you need to shift the time, that's fine-it's your business, so do what's bestfor you.

Then, when you've finished those calls, send *two* emails to the same type of people, say one email to a real estate agent and one to a past referral partner or current referral partner. Again, just be conversational in your email, because you're simply checking in, and planting a seed with them to think about you.

After that, write *one* post on social media.

My recommendation is to spread out your posts-say Facebook on Monday, and LinkedIn on Tuesday, and maybe Twitter on Wednesday, maybe something on Zillow on Thursday, that type of thing. Don't post in the same place every single day.

To get started to eventually calling ten people every day, start with three phone calls, send two emails, and post one article on social media. Now if even this is too much for you to start, think about doing 1-1-1. One phone call, one email, one social post. Maybe you only want to do one phone call and leave it at that. After all, it's the same process as reaching the goal of 10 pushups, especially if you haven't done any pushups for a few years. You simply do one the first day, then two the second day, and before you know it you're up to ten a day.

There you have it. If you're not ready or able to make ten calls every day, get going with the 3-2-1 system. No matter how you get started or how many calls you make, absolutely make your outgoing, lead-generation phone calls your first priority every morning.

Jen'sJots

♦ Can't make ten 1st and 10 phone calls every day starting on Day 1? Then start out with a plan that is comfortable for you.

♦ Think about starting with three phone calls, two emails, and one social media post every day. Even a 1-1-1 plan will start paying dividends.

♦ However you get started, do it now!

✳ Before We Hang Up: The One Last Question

> **The Big Idea:** *There is a simple way to grow the size of your network and database every single day and there is no extra work involved Just ask this quick question at the end of each of your phone calls*
>
> *"When one door of opportunity closes, another opens; but often we look so long at the closed door that we do not see the one which has been opened for us"*
>
> *- Helen Keller*

It's a constant struggle, A dark cloud hanging over your head, following you around, It's the pressure you feel to build your referral network,

I can see what you're doing to try to build your network of partners, You careen from one pursuit to another, trying to make connections that lead to referral part ner relationships that lead to potential business, You go to networking events, business mixers, seminars, open-houses, *anything* to make more connections,

Stop bouncing around like a pinball! There's a much, much easier way to con stantly grow the size of your network, and the beauty of it is, you don't have to do anything extra than you're already doing! You can increase the size of your network quite literally every day and on practically every phone call you make, You just ask one quick question at the end of every call. That's all there is to it. And like magic, your network and your connections grow by leaps and bounds,

I suppose you want to know what this magic question is!

It's simply this, And that end of the call, after you've wrapped up your business and conversation, ask the following question: "Before we hang up, can you rec ommend a *good{fill in the blankF"*

Be Specific

So, what is it you're asking? Well, what's your goal? You're looking for ways to increase the size of your network. This may be your network of real estate agents, financial planners, attorneys, and other professionals who intersect with your potential clients. Or you may be looking to build up your network of home services providers such as plumbers, contractors, deck builders, and the like so that you can be a resource for your clients, or perhaps you are growing your team or searching for a specific type of client.

Use the "Before we hang up" question-or your variation of it-to identify a *specific* type of potential partner or clien\ele. Be very precise about what you're look ing for. This is not the time to be vague!

Let me walk you through the conversation. Let's say you're talking with a pros pect, and you're about readyto end the conversation. At that point you say, "Oh, gosh, before we hang up, I am looking to expand my business in the arena of working with financial advisors. I was wondering if you have a great financial advisor who you would feel comfortable introducing me to?"

Another example is, "Hey, before we hang up, I'm always trying to add to my list of home service professionals thatI can share with my clients. Do you happen to know a great landscaper?"

And justlikethat (sound of fingers snapping), you have a lead on a potential refer ral partner or home service provider.

Create a Daily or Weekly Target

Let's get back to the part about being specific.

Think through the areas where you really want more quality connections, andthen plan a weekly or even a daily target to identify that specific type of connection.

If you're looking to connect with more real estate agents who serve a particular niche or clientele-be specific. If you're looking to connect with more financial planners-that'swhat you ask for that week.

Commit to a target, write it down,and ask *aboutjustthat target* for a week. Then move on to another target the next week.

Be focused and systematic about using this question. Your resultswillbe amazing.

Closing the Loop

Of course, I did fib a little. It's a *very* simple technique, but it's not *that* simple of a process.

Now that you have a name or a lead, you will need to reach out and introduce yourself or ask the person you're talking with if they canfacilitate an introduction, especially if the prospective contact is a referral partner. Barring that, ask if you can use their name when you call the prospective partner.

From there, go through the process you would go through with any new referral partner. After you connect, meet with them in a one-to-one to explore if you have a common interest in working together. If so, fantastic. Add them to your referral partner database, and put them into your regular cycle of partner meetings and daily phone calls.

Then, the next time you have a phone conversation with this new partner, you can ask them, "Say, before we hang up ..." See how this just builds on itself over time? You'll find the number of your connections growing by leaps and bounds. As you work with and communicate with this ever-growing network of connections, many, many opportunities for new business will come your way.

See. It is like magic!

Why This Works So Well

This is such an easy question to ask. It doesn't make the other person uncom fortable. It doesn't put them on the spot. I know that sometimes as loan officers we're afraid to ask for the business. But in this case, we're simply asking for a *connection.*

I'm a big advocate of not always asking for the *fish.* Think of this as asking to con nect to someone who knows where there might be a good place to fish.

You don't want to be in the situation where you feel forced to ask at the end of *every* call, "Hey, before we hang up, can you recommend someone you know who might be buying or selling a home and who needs financing?" Asking that all day long, day after day, will deflate you. And fast.

Now, there are circumstances where you will want to ask that question directly. But if you're new to the business you may feel you're being pushy. (Believe me, it can be difficult for people who've been in the industry for many years to ask for business too.) Eventually, you'll get to the point where you're asking for business when the circumstances are right.

In the meantime, use this simple "Before we hang up ..." question to expand your network and get connected to more referral partners. With more connections, you can increase your value proposition to referral partners *and* provide more value to your clients.

Make It Natural

Put some effort into making this question a natural-sounding part of your conver sation.

Ask the question in your own words and style. Maybe you'd prefer to say something like, "Say, there's just one more thing..." or, "Let me ask you a quick question before we end..." or some variation. Make it your own and put it in your words.

Script it if you have to. No, really. Write it down and have it in front of you when you make phone calls until it becomes ingrained in your DNA.

Before you start using it, practice it in your mind. Rehearse it, out loud, behind closed doors. Get so comfortable with the question that it simply flows as a natural extension of your conversation.

Use this question over and over. I promise your universe will expand constantly and at an accelerated rate.

Jen's Jots

♦ Use a simple question beginning with "Before we hang up..." to expand your database and/or network of referral partners and clients.

♦ Ask this question at the end of every one of your daily 1st and 10 phone calls.

♦ Be very specific, and use a daily or weekly target.

♦ For example, if you want to increase your business in the arena of working with financial planners, you would say, "Before we hang up, I'm expanding my mortgage practice to include working directly with financial planners. Do you happen to know of a great planner that you could introduce me to?"

✳ Replace It, Don't Erase It

> **The Big Idea:** When something important such as a closing conflicts with a business-building activity you have on your daily calendar, don't erase that activity, Move it to another block within your schedule on the same day so your business-building efforts are consistent.
>
> *"The story of life is written in ink, not pencil. You can't go back and erase the past so live for today and make good choices for tomorrow."*
>
> *-Anonymous*

One thing that really keeps your business moving forward and growing is consis tency, Any top producer that you talk to will tell youthat they consistently do the same things over and over, They don't get really excited about some new thing and do it for a week or two, and then drift away from it. Consistent application is what setsyou up for success.

Think about this in sports terms, Love him or hate him, Tom Brady is the perfect example of consistent application, His experience shows that consistent practice, study, and training will lead to long-term success. Would he still be playing football at an extremely highlevel at 40 years of age if he didn't consistently work on his preparation? It's unlikely.

So consistency in what you're doing makes you better. And yes, it might feel mundane because you're saying the same scripts over and over and doing the same things over and over. But I promise you,it's going to make your business extremely successful.

This is especially true when applying principles of time compression to your schedule.

Let's sayyou're applying the practice of time compression, and you're trying to be consistent about it. But an issue comes up, and it's something that I'm finding happens to my coaching clients and others I talk to. What do you do when a clos ing occurs from 9:00to 10:00 on any given day and that is the time you have set aside for your 1st and 10 phone calls?

If a closing comes up that interferes with your 1st and 10 phone calls do you say you're sorry,I can't go to the closing because I have an appointment? Of course not,youwant to go to the settlement.

But what do you do about your daily phone calls? Do you forget about them for that day? Do you try to double up the number of calls you make the next day? Do you try to slot in an hour somewhere next week?

Instead of erasing that time for the day,I strongly encourage you to replace that time somewhere during the same day. If you can't make the calls from 9:00 to 10:00 because of a settlement, then make the calls from 11:00 to noon or from 3:00 to 4:00.

The key is, don't erase that block off your schedule and don't take it off your activities for the day. Put this important activity elsewhere on your schedule for the day to develop day-to-day consistency. The key is to still make the calls *that* day.What ends up happening when you erase akey business-building activity off your calendar is it never gets done.If you repeat this for a few days,you willbegin to drift away from your goals.

Well,you say,just a little drifting away from my plan won't really hurt me. But think about it this way: Let's say a plane is flying from Las Vegas to Boston and it drifts off course consistently every hour by just one-half a degree. What would happen? Well, it would miss Boston! Just like the plane,what may seem like minor drifts, minor adjustments, minor "erasings" that you do every now and then will cause you to go off-course and miss your goal. The problem is that you won't know you've drifted until later,when it's too late to make a course adjustment.

The more you erase things from your time blocks and don't replace them on the same day,the more inconsistent you will become. The more inconsistent you are, the more likely you are to go off course and not hit your goals. Then you wonder why you're not as successful as you want to be. You wonder why your numbers are lower one month,then higher,onlyto drop again.

Inco nsistency in your effort is what can cause these peaks and valleys. You develop a lot of business through consistent business-building activities andthen when the loans come in you slack off. The issue is at the end of the month when allthe loans have dosed,you then have fewer loans closing the nextmonth. Then you get more consistent about doing your business-buildingactivities again, and it becomes an endless cycle of ups and downs.

It's important to remember thatif youcan't get to something that is on your sched ule-aside from the fact that I'll always stress that you should stick to a sched ule-don't just erase it from your calendar. Replace it the same day so you remain consistent. Trying to move a business-building activity to a different day will take you off track. I promise you it will,because if you tell yourself, 'Well,tomorrow, I'll make phone calls for two hours;· it's likelyyou won't. Then you'll be drifting even farther.

Erasing the calls from your schedule is the same as Tom Brady saying, "I'm not going to practice throwing today or tomorrow but what I'll do is onThursday I'll throw for six hours." But what would happen? His arm might be sore and he's going to take longer to recover, and maybe he won't play as well in the next game.

That will happen to you,too. You don't want to try to cram everything in by dou bling up. This will cause you even more stress, and you may even have twice the follow-up to complete the calls, which will of course interfere with your next planned activity.

People say to me, 'Tm trying this time blocking but it's not working!" That's because they are encountering these occasional conflicts and rather than replace an activity within the same day, they're trying to cram the missed activity into another day. That leads to inconsistency and ultimately giving up.

Jen's Jots

♦ When a closing or other important event conflicts with a daily business building activity, move that activity to a different part of the day. Don't erase it from your schedule.

♦ Carry out your business-building activities every day to create consistency in achieving your goals.

✳ Before, During, and After

> **The Big Idea:** *Every meeting with a referral partner or potential partner is important. Create and follow systems to ensure you are prepared Before, During, and After each meeting.*
>
> *"Proper Planning Prevents Poor Performance."*
>
> *- The 5 Ps of Sales*

Just as you should blueprint your day, you should also blueprint or prepare diligently for any and every meeting you have and for any follow-up steps you need to take after a meeting.

Focus on what you will be doing *Before, During,* and *After* (BDA) a meeting by creating and following a system.

Think about some of your recent meetings (and here's hoping you've had some recent meetings with partners and potential partners). Were there times when you weren't well prepared so you didn't present yourself to the best of your profes sional ability? Did you follow up after every single meeting? Did you even think about following up?

I call the lack of following up after a meeting the One-and-Done Syndrome. You have a meeting and then no matter how positive it was,well ...nothing happens, you're done. What a waste of time! You leave the meeting having agreed thatyou will start doing business together and then never talk to the person again.

Start now-I mean this minute-by approaching each meeting with a purpose and by creating a system for following up. This is one of the keys to my success. But I'm going to be honest, it does take time to build and it won't be set in stone. Great systems remain fluid to adjust to market conditions and changes.

Visualize a meeting you have on your schedule. What specific steps might you want to take *Before, During,* and *After* to be prepared, to be fully present, and then to follow up? Let me run through some examples for you-these are not comprehensive by any means just a way to help you get started and create your own systems.

Before:

- Do you need to do some research on the person you are meeting?
- What collateral might you need to prepare?
- Do you know exactly where you are meeting them?
- Do you want to send them something in advance of the meeting via email, snail mail, or stop by in person?

During:

- Think through how you want the meeting to go. What questions do you want to ask?
- What is the goal of the meeting?
- Are you presenting something?
- How will you be able to help their business?
- Have you practiced your elevator speech?
- Are you prepared for any objections and how to overcome them?

After

- When will you enter them into your contact database?
- Who will do the entering?
- What will you do to follow up?
- Have you given yourself enough wiggle room in your calendar to actually do the follow-up you promised?
- How will you deliver?
- How often will you follow up and by what means (email, social media, in person, phone, mail, etc.)?

Createa System for Follow-up Communication

After holding my first meeting with a referral partner, I communicate with them seven times over the course of 70 days. Every 10 days- just as they are about to forget me-I getin touch with them in one of several ways. I email something that is of interest to them personally or in their business, call them to check in (this is one of my 1st & 10 calls), stop by their office, make a social media connec tion, send them my monthly newsletter (snail mail and email), video text, write a personal note, or send a success story. After 70 days, if we are not working together, we never will! I move on. NOTE: I do, however, keep them in my com munity database.

Action Steps You Can Take

Here are some action steps you can take to prepare Before, During, and After:

◆ Think through what you want to accomplish in your meetings. Create and/ or print your collateral for meetings. Maybe this would include a question naire or interview sheet so that you can remember everything you want to ask.

◆ *Grab a colleague and role-play your meetings. How will you ask ques tions, by reading your interview sheet or casually looking at it? (I use the **FROG** technique to ask about their Family, Recreation, Occupation, and Goals.)*

◆ *What if there is an objection to your proposition? Develop responses to overcome anything that could possibly arise!*

◆ *Make a list of all the things you could do to keep in touch with someone (see the sidebar for ideas). Add ideas that work for you. Use those ways to communicate in an order that makes sense for you. I typically start with a personal note, but there's nothing to prevent you from starting with, say, a social media connection.*

Jen's Jots

◆ Approach every meeting with a purpose and a plan and create a system for effective follow-up after the meeting.

◆ Visualize specific actions you might want to take Before, During, and After to be prepared, to be present, and then to follow up.

◆ Create a system to implement follow-up communication with a potential partner after your first meeting.

✳ Stack 'em Up

> **The Big Idea:** Leverage more benefits and value from your meetings with
> referral partners by having a weekly Stacking Day.
> "If you're going to be married to your excuses..
> it's time to divorce your dreams!"
>
> - Jen Du Plessis

I'm always looking for ways to get maximum benefit and value out of my time compressed daily calendar. One way I do this is by having a weekly *Stacking Day* in my time-blocked schedule.

It sounds like I'm piling on more work, but I'm not. What I'm actually doing is lever aging consecutive meetings with partners to create more connections and value for my partners. And this increases my value to them!

I began this practice a little over four years ago and haven't stopped since. In fact, several of my referral partners sometimes now ask me, "Am I being **stacked** at this meeting?" They know that being stacked means they are going to be intro ducedto someone who maybenefit the expansion of their business.

Here's how it works. On my *Stacking Day,* I schedule consecutive meetings with three of my referral partners at the same location. My usual schedule is meeting number 1at 11:00 a.m., meeting number 2 at noon, and meeting number 3 at 1:00 p.m.

My goal in having mymeetings back-to-back-to-back is to be able to introduce my referral partner at meeting #1to my referral partner at meeting #2 and my referral partner at meeting #2 to my referral partner at meeting #3. I try to match partners so the introduction will benefit them and their business. For example, I might introduce a real estate agent to a divorce attorney and thenthe divorce attorney to an estate planner. Of course, you need to know enough about your referral partners to know who they want to be connected with (remember the questions to ask when meeting partners!).

I make sure that what I plan to talk about during each of the meetings can be wrapped up in about 50 minutes. When the partner for meeting #2 arrives, I can easily and quickly make the introduction as the partner from meeting #1is leav ing. As I said, you will need to have learned enough about your referral partners to know who they want to meet or know about their personal needs and goals.

The Logistics

To get your *Stacking Day* underway, book a reservation at a local "nice" restau rant from 11:00 am to 2:00 pm. You will have to locate one that opens at 11:00 to accommodate your first meeting. Let them know that you would like a standing reservation for everyweek on the same day. You can also give restaurant staff the names of the partners who will be coming to meet you. The staff will be glad to assist you by letting you know when your next guest has arrived or bringing the person to your table.

Be sure to be nice to the restaurant staff and also tip them well! This will pay off in great service and you may also reap some extra benefits. I've received a gift certificate and several free lunches, and even better, I've closed three loans as a result of referrals from the staff!

Think of the people you can make appointments with. Which of them could you turn into a stacking appointment? Who would they like to meet? What other type of business could benefit theirs? Here's another example: Introduce an HVAC contractor to a builder and thenthe builder to a cleaning company or stager.

In your stacking days, involve both current partners and those you are seeking to make your partners. You'll demonstrate how you can provide value by introducing them to people who will help their business. Your current partners will be testi mony enough, and this will help grow your business too.

Jen'sJots

♦ Schedule three one-hour meetings with referral partners back-to-back-to back once a week.

♦ Book a standing reservation at a local restaurant that canaccommodate a schedule of meetings from 11:00 a.m. to 2:00 p.m.

♦ Match partners at consecutive meetings who may benefit from meeting one another. You add value to their business and make yourself a stronger partner in the process.

✳ The Networking Bottom-Line

> **The Big Idea:** *Do some preparation ahead of a networking event. This will ensure you will make at least one good connection. After all, that's your goal.*
>
> *"Don't confuse efforts with results"*
>
> *- Tom Barrack*

Do you ever get tired of going to networking events and feeling like it was a waste of time? If that's the case, then do some groundwork before you go to make sure that every event you attend results in one QUALITY connection to help you grow, expand, or expose your practice.

I hear constantly from loan officers that sooo many people are involved in sooo many networking events and groups,but the results just aren't there. It's become the Art of being Busy. When we start looking at the results and actually tracking the contacts made at each event, we find that with the amount of time wasted and energy spent,the consequences for attending these events is loss of money.

Let me see if I can shed some light. You can attend a networking event or sit on a committee and be the mortgage person and never get business. It's your job to make the connection and ask for business to teach them to begin thinking about you for their connections as well. What is networking? Well, it isn't a place to get business! You get names and business cards from networking-it's how youuse them. Go to them or people will forget about you. But business is not generated from merely showing up, and in fact I've found that people who are at all the events tend to be the people not doing any business.

Recently I was coaching one of my clients and we started looking at all the differ ent networking events that she was attending. She admitted that she was leaving a lot of the events without any business cards at all. Not one! So, she was literally going to these things as a social function and not a work function. I callthis "cock tail conversations." There mayin fact be a few situations where you go to an event for the social side of networking, but that's really a party, right,not a networking or business event.

Authenticity and Truth

Go to networking events where you are true to yourself. Please don't attend an eventjust because someone asked you. Think through this and employ the tech niques we've been discussing. Are you acting as a "yes" man or woman? Will one of your bestreferral partners or clients be attending or going withyou? In my experience, and I'll betyours too, whenever I've attended an event that I really didn't want to, or that was for a topic or cause I didn't care about or wasn't pas sionate about,I felt completely out of place. And believe me, people can see and feel it.

When we are authentic, people are drawn to us and this becomes a launching point for building a relationship. Finding your niche and working within the con fines of it is understanding that thisis a marathon, not a sprint. You must be patient and tenacious withthe process.

Check Attendees Aheadof Time

The key to making each and every networking event a successful event-and by success, I mean leaving with at least one solid, new *connection-is* in laying some groundwork ahead of time. Then you can go for the right reasons. Networking is not about "getting business;· it is 100 percent about making connections!

So,in this particular client's case she was signing up for anything and everything to get the exposure. My opinion is that you don't want to go to every single event possible if you don't know who's going to be attending or what your purpose is for attending.

First check to see who is attending. It's important to know the audience that's going to be going to the event. If you're fortunate enough to have access to an Eventbrite or Facebook invitation, it's very easyto see who's going and who's not going to be attending. You can look at their profiles and find out a little bit about them.

If you don't have an opportunity to check on attendees through an online tool,you can contact the organizer of the event. You can simply say to them, "You know I'm thinking about coming to the event,I'd love to come and contribute and help make your event a success, but I'm wondering if you could give me a list of who's attending or if you could just walk through a list with me of who's attending. Who I'm looking for is (fill in the blank]." And describe the kind of connection you are looking for. So, for example, let the person know that you're looking for financial planners. Do financial planners typically come to the event? If not, well, maybe that's an event you don't go to. Maybe it is. Do small business owners attend? Let's say, for example, that you want to do a seminar series for small business owners on how to get ready for qualifying for a loan andyou wantto meet several business owners. Then ask the organizer about what kind of business people attend. Are they mostly business owners who will be coming to this event, or is it mostly business development and sales people? Are they from large companies or small companies?

There is a great variety of reasons why you want to know who is attending and how that affects the dynamics of your goals for attending.

Get a Warm Introduction

When you go to the event, don't try to get a business card from every Tom, Dic k, and Harry. Make the event worth your while by making a minimum of connections to follow up with.

One way to ensure this is to get the organizer's assistance in meeting a target connection. Let's say that when you talk to the organizer you find that someone you have been targeting and have wanted to meet or someone who fits into the category of where you're trying to expand your business will be attending. Then by all means, ask the organizer if they can make a personal introduction for you. When you get to the event, go to the organizer and ask them to point out the particular person you're seeking and to introduce you. This way you're not trying to find a needle in a haystack at a crowded networking event, not knowing who the person is. You won't face the prospect of walking up to someone cold and catching them off-guard. You'll get a warm introduction, which is more likely to lead to a five- or ten-minute conversation. You can have a conversation about their business, not a "pitch" conversation, but just a conversation to learn about them. Your goal is to follow-up after the networking event to schedule a one-to one meeting; even better if you can schedule it right there on the spot. If you feel there could be a profitable connection, ask them right then if it would be possible if you could schedule a coffee so that you could see if there's an opportunity for you to work together.

That is your main goal: To meet one or two people that you specifically want to meet. After that, it's all gravy. You can socialize, you can try to meet more connec tions, or you can leave. Mission accomplished!

I have found that this technique works very well. I don't know how many times early in my career that I left a networking event and said to myself, "You know what, why did I even go? Why did I sit in traffic? Why did I come here for an hour and a half and waste my time?" I learned quite quickly that if I just communicate with the organizer, I can almost guarantee the event will be a success for me.

I've also found that "buddying up" with someone you already know will increase the chances that you'll make a new connection. If you know someone who's going to the same event, let them know who you're looking for and ask who they're looking for. Then you'll both have your ears open and your antennas up during the event for each other so that you can do warm introductions for one another.

The buddy system has been truly successful for me, and I do it these days to help other people. The primary thing I do is get in touch with the organizer or find a list of who's going to a networking event and make it a point to meet the one person or a couple of people I want to meet.

Follow-up When You Say You Will

You've made at least one solid connection at a networking event. That's great!

Now leave yourself some "white space" after the event for following up. If the event is in the evening and you want to follow-up to do a one-to-one with some one, or you said you'd send some information or call them, then make sure the next morning that you follow-up in the first hour you're in the office. Don't go to a networking event one evening and then have a breakfast the next day with back to-back meetings knowing that you can't commit to something you told some one at the networking event. Just be aware of that. Make sure you have some white space behind it, somewhere, so that you can utilize that time to follow-up effectively. If you fail to call when you said you would, then time will pass and eventually you won't call at all. And if so, why did you even bother going to the networking event in the first place? Mission not accomplished!

Jen's Jots

♦ Create better opportunities at every networking event you attend by find ing out who else will be attending and if a particular person or type of person you want to meet will be there.

♦ Ask an event's organizer to introduce you to a specific person you are seeking. This warm introduction will lead to a more profitable conversa tion.

✳ Just the "Text" Ma'am

> **The Big Idea:** Use group texting on your smartphone to stay top of mind with your partners and clients
>
> *"The greatest definition for concentration I ever heard is, 'Wherever you are, be there!'"*
>
> *-JimRohn*

Today's easy-to-use communication technology tools are great resources for reaching out to your network,keeping in touch, and helping to make sure referrals keep flowing. A very handy tool that I've started to make use of is group texting.

I use group texting to stay in touch with defined groups of partners and clients-such as the real estate agents I work with the most-which has generated new business for me time and time again,

Now, let me say that before you get into the nuts-and-bolts of sending out a group text,make sure you have a purpose as to why you're doing it, then use it from a strategic marketing perspective. You can use group texting strategically to stay top of mind with target groups of partners, to provide value to partners and clients, and to enhance connections and communication. There are many ways to creatively and unobtrusively use group texting which will help keep leads and prospects coming in,

What to Do

The first thing you need to send a group text is to download an app on your smartphone, Do a quick search and you'll find there are many apps to choose from. Once you've downloaded the app,you can upload his may happen auto matically) all of the contacts on your phone. Then, you can set up your target distribution lists, such as just your top real estate agent partners, "B" partners, or all real estate agent partners, Then you can compose one text,hit "send;' and it will be delivered to all members of a distribution list or group.

Once you have the app downloaded and the groups set up, make a commitment as to when you're going to send a text and to whom, Maybe you want to do a weekly text, a monthly text, maybe a quarterly text to various groups. What I'm doing, for example, is sending a text weekly either Thursday afternoon or Friday morning to all of my A-plus referral real estate agents. The rest of my real estate agent contacts get a text once a month at the beginning of the month. (Don't send a text at the end of the month because agents will be too busy and won't pay attention.)

I have found that sending a text toward the end of the week is much better than the first of the week, because during the first part of the week I'm making phone calls and touching base live. But Thursday or Friday is a good time to send a text out to everybody. What you want to make sure of is that you keep the text generic because you're sending it to a multiple people. Be generic, yet just spe cific enough so that everyone feels like you are textingjust them and not a group of people; that is a key point.

Your texts should be very short, like a tweet.

What to Say

The next step is to determine what you're going to say in the text.

I have sent texts that are personal and friendly, such as sharing whether I'm going to be in town or out of town for the weekend. I've even sent a message about something that I'm planning on doing and how excited I am to have the weekend come along. I think that your real estate agents would love hearing about what you're doing, as it puts a personal touch on your business relationship.

I've also sent texts that offer some value to my agent contacts, such as quick reminders about specific types of loans, or reminders about what has happened with interest rates during the week andwhat that might mean for their clients. I'm not repeating information they can find in the news, but I'm just reminding them, for example, that rates have gone up a little bit during the week so if they have anyone who is sitting on the fence it maybe time to get a commitment from them. Or maybe rates went down so I remind them that now's a great time to get buyers off the fence and into their homes and let's strike while the iron is hot.

Quick event reminders are always a greatthing to text.I've sent reminders about seminars I have coming up, or that I'm going to be speaking at an event and I'd love to have them attend, or that I'm having a business mixer and just wanted to check in and see if theywere planning on coming to it.

As you're going through the week, anytime you have questions from clients it's a great opportunity to write those down and make one the topic of thatweek's text.

Group texting has also worked for me in reconnecting with some people who, for whatever reason, haven't been responsive to my regular phone calls or emails. After receiving one of my texts they've replied and said, "Oh gosh, it's great to hear from you, let's get some coffee." It's been great for rekindling my relation ships as well.

I've created other groups: a list of prospects, a list of my past clients or closed clients, a list of my clients in process, and a list of my certified financial planners. Now I can text these groups as well. For example, I'm sending prospects little tidbits about credit, the loan process, a link about interest rates, or just checking in to see how their house-hunting is going. For loans that are currently in process, I might send a quick text to let clients know that if they have any questions over an upcoming weekend what would be the best way to reach me. Again, it's a very simple text that looks like I'm sending it just to that one individual.

Group texts can show some immediate results. One of the texts I sent was just a reminder to a real estate agent list that I can provide financing outside of my state. And, oh my gosh, what a great response. Right after sending that text I received a response from one of my real estate agent partners who was in South Carolina and was about to make an offer on a second home for herself. I'm happy to say that I ended up closing her loan and I am just tickled about how that worked.

Find Your Level of Comfort

Now, you need decide what frequency of texting is right for you. For me, sending something every week to certain groups of partners is too much. It's about what works best for you and what you want to accomplish with this tool. I would at minimum suggest a group text weekly to your A-plus partners so you can regularly remind them that you're available to support their business and to your current clients so they know you're totally involved in their transactions. You will find more business coming your way if you keep at this consistently.

Jen's.Jots

♦ Decide on a strategy of how you can use a group texting app to keep you front and center with your partners.

♦ Follow a plan and schedule for how often you send a text, to whom, and what the topic will be.

✳ Set Expectations with Clients for Referrals

> **The Big Idea:** From the very beginning of your relationship with a client, start educating them about how your practice thrives through referrals Begin nurturing their awareness of how they will discover referable clients
>
> *"Unexpected extras only work if you do the expected first!"*
>
> *-Anonymous*

If you're waiting until the loan approval or closing to askfor a referral, you're miss ing some golden opportunities to get clients thinking about referrals, You should set expectations for referrals from the veryfirstmeeting with a client.

I find that most loan officers don't ask for referrals from clients until the loan is approved. You know, way back,we thought thatwas the best time to askfor refer rals from borrowers, when their love-o-meter was at its peak and they're happy withyou because you just provided them with a loan approval.

And while I think that's a great time to askfor a referral, and it is incorporated into my process as well, quite frankly I think approval is a little too late for the initial ask. Now the nextplace that I see loan officers asking for referrals is at the actual closing or escrow. Again, a great place and I do that,but I think it'sjust a little too late to star/asking. Your client is only thinking about moving into their new home, not about sendingyou a referral.

Build Awareness Immediately

Let me share withyou a way that youcan set expectations with a client from the moment you meet them, whether it's in person or on the phone, to ensure that they understand how important referrals are to you. What you want to do is help beginthinking throughout their *entire* loan process about providing referrals.

You know, clients don't understand how we're paid, and they also don't under stand how we get business. It's our job to help them understand our expectations. The first step I take when I meet with a client is to push all of the paperwork aside. You know how they are,they come in and they're so excited to give us all this documentation andwe're so excited to tell them all about us and show the graphs and product selections we've prepared.

I want to push all that aside and just have a conversation with them. What that may sound like is, "I'm so excited to meet with you, thank you for coming into my office today. You know, before we get started I want to just stop for a few minutes and take this opportunity to get to know each other a bit better. And, so if you don't mind, can we take just a few minutes to let me share about my practice and how I operate?"

Now I will tell you I've never had anyone say to me, "No, you can't do that. I just want the numbers, I'm not interested in that." They really do want to know, so all you have to do is just ask them. This builds great trust!

The second part of this is then talking about how you work by referral. By remind ing them that even their real estate agent introduced them to you, you demon strate through their own situation how you work by referral.

What you're doing is planting the seed immediately that you are looking for refer rals, and you're doing that right from the very beginning. Of course, you can't plant a seed and just hope that it grows, you have to constantly water it. And that's why you will want to constantly put information in front of them or while on the phone with them throughout the process to remind them that you do work by referral.

Talk About Expectations

I tell my clients that my job is to "Wow" them throughout the loan process so that they're compelled to talk about me. I tell them that my goal is to exceed their expectations so that they *want* to talk about me and introduce me to people that they know.

Now listen, you have to find out what their expectations are so that you can actu ally exceed them. You can't exceed expectations that you're not clear about!

How do they want to be communicated with? Do they want texts, do they want phone calls, do they want emails? Do they want you to talk to the husband and not the wife or vice versa? Are there other people who are going to be involved in the decision-making, like a father or mother, or a trusted advisor or referral partner, a potential referral partner?

Each of these points are important as you take a breath, step back, and talk about the relationship rather than assuming through the whole process that you will get referrals.

Another suggestion when talking with them is, "Let me share with you about what to expect during the loan process." You're going to subconsciously start noticing and becoming aware that a lot of people you know and talk to are also thinking abou t buying a home or refinancing or are talking abou t a mortgage. It's a very common thing, much like noticing after you buy a red car how many red cars you'll suddenly see on the road."

You want to let them know that during their loan process you're asking them to keep their antennas up for people they might introduce to you. You've already asked and mentioned a few times that you work by referral and now you're plant ing with them, slowly but surely, not a hard-core sale, but an awareness that they're going to recognize other people in the same situation more often. You're nurturing the message that you want them to be looking out for you while you are being held accountable for exceeding their expectations.

Now, the other important part of talking about your practice is to explain to them how you want to be referred. For example, I do not like being referred to as a mortgage broker, as a loan officer, as "my lender girl," or as "my loan person." I make it clear how I prefer to be referred to, and because I have the designation of Certified Mortgage Planner it's important for me that they use that terminology. So whatever terminology you want them to use for you, you need to explain to them.

That's really easy to do, you just ask them, "Is there anything you would need from me to help you explain me and my practice to others?" Just ask them, then give them some ideas to use with anyone they're referring.

You also want to make sure that people know you are referable and you want to be accepting of referrals. It is imperative for your client to understand that there is never a time when you're not accepting referrals. And you want to express this while you're sitting with them. You're making sure that there 's nothing else they need from you to explain to others who you are, your practice's operation, and what kind of experience these friends and family will get when they are referred to you.

You Can Ask Right Away

Then the last step is to use the same script addressed in chapter 4-10 after all your phone calls, the "Before we hang up" line. In this case, however, you can say "Before we go," and ask for a connection in the same way you ask during your phone calls.

This is a perfect opportunity for you to ask for a referral right then and there. By the way, the referral does not have to be a direct referral of another client buy ing a home. It can be a referral for a connection to a potential partner or service provider. This will help them ease into the referral process.

Of course, you can ask for a direct referral by saying something such as, "Hey, before we go, I'm always looking to work with other expecting couples just like you," or, "I'm always looking to work with other women who are going through a divorce just like you who might need my assistance, guidance, and expertise to help them through the process. Who do you know in the same situation as you whom you would feel comfortable introducing me to?"

When youcall them when their appraisal comes in, andwhen the loan is approved and you're about ready to go to closing, or at closing, you can feel more comfortable asking for a referral. You've set expectations from the very beginning of your relationship.

A Processfor AllSituations

This technique is so powerful and so easy to do at every appointment you have, for example,with real estate agents.

You want to let the agents know that your job is to wow them, in the same way you do for your clients, and exceed their expectations. Ask about the other loan officers that they're working with.What do they do well? What don't they do well? What does this real estate agent wish that the loan officers they're working with, if they are, could do better so that you can exceed their expectations? I promise you that other loan officers are not asking these questions. You can also ask them, "Is there anything thatyou need from me to be able to explain my loan process or about how my team operates?" At the end of the conversation, you can certainly add in the "Oh,before we go" question.

You can use this referral creator strategy in any situation that you're in, any one to-one meeting or any phone call or appointment that you have.

When you do this,your business will grow because now you're continually plant ing the seed to bring in referrals. If you follow up diligently after you've planted this seed andwater it so that it grows,your business will grow through referrals. If you don'twater that seed and you just put it in the ground and you walk away and simply hope and wish and maybe pray that you get referrals, then that's exactly
what you're going to get-just hopes and wishes.

Jen's Jots

◆ Don't wait until the closing to start asking for referrals. By then you've missed out on many opportunities to ask for referrals.

◆ From the beginning of your relationship, take a few minutes to educate new dients about how your practice works and how you get your business through referrals.

◆ During the entire loan process,constantly nurture a client's mindfulness of potential clients they might refer.

◆ Use this same process and technique with real estate agents and other partners.

✳ Scoring Big with Your Clients

> **The Big Idea:** *Share the goodnews with a borrower when they receive loan approval by stopping by their workplace with something they can share with their coworkers and which calls attention to your practice.*
>
> *"If you are not willing to risk the unusual,*
> *you will have to settle for the ordinary."*
>
> *-JimRohn*

You do a great job for your clients, that's a given. But do you keep them at arm's length rather than really leaning in and striking up a bond that might last through a second or even a third loan somewhere down the road? Do they forget about you as they're walking out the door after their closing, or do theytake a piece of you with them?

Now,I'm not suggesting you need to get chummy or buddy-buddy. I am suggest ing you do things a little differently, that you do something unexpected and per sonal to make yourself memorable. Do something beyond offering great seNice and solving any problems that crop up in the mortgage process.

Let me give you one idea.We typically sendthank-you notes and other marketing material to clients' homes, right? But have you ever thought of dropping by their work location to do a warm sales call face-to face? And have you also thought about the fact that they most likely have colleagues thatyou could meet?

Visiting your borrower's office is a great way to elevate your service and image in your client's eyes. Now, you obviously need a reason to make this visit, and there is a perfect opportunity that occurs during every successful loan process: the loan approval.

During the entire loan process, your borrower will go through times of highs and lows, and their love-o-meter, as I like to call it, can fluctuate considerably. The borrower may love you when you first take their loan application. But as time goes on, the love-o-meter starts wavering a little bit. You can also call this their trust account. At the beginning their trust account is full,but thenthey start taking withdrawals because you may not be calling them back or you're not updating them on their loan progress or what the next steps will be, or you're not explaining why you need the droves and droves of paperwork required in our industry today.

115

In our industry there are three times when our clients love us the most: when they make the decision to work with us, when they get loan approval, and when they go to closing (assuming everything goes well).

As a result, the love-a-meter or trust account fluctuates. In order to keep the rela tionship strong you always want to be leaning into your business and not waiting for your business to happen. Again, in other chapters I've talked about the differ ence between defensive and offensive phone calls. It's the same here; when you lean in it's an offensive move and increases the love or makes a deposit in the trust account. Your client will appreciate you being proactive. When you have a lack of communication you are sure to lose the opportunity for future referrals.

When their loan is approved, you have a great opportunity to stop by your client's office. This is when their love-a-meter is the highest because they're happy; the loan is approved and you're ready to start moving toward closing. What better opportunity than to drop by their office with a gift that recognizes the importance of the moment for them and that they can share with their coworkers? In your client's eyes, you'll differentiate yourself as someone who cares, and of course there's the side benefit of getting recognition and attention from coworkers.

Cake, and Balloons, and Congratulations

Let me give you two quick ideas on what you could do when you stop by their office.

You can certainly stop by without any type of a gift, just to say "Congratulations," and that you just wanted to see the expression on their face when you gave them the news. What I do is stop by strategically with the clients that I feel could have a bigger impact on my business; that is, those who are more likely to refer. And perhaps, but not always, they might be working in a larger company where they have more opportunities to refer. Additionally, I typically send the approval gift to the most "chatty" client when there are two of them.

I like to stop by with a cake (or send a cake) that says "Congratulations!" on it, accompanied by balloons and ribbons and, of course, tons of my business cards. Now the reason I do this is because it will attract attention from lots of coworkers. Just a side note: due to privacy concerns you may want to be careful not to say, "Congratulations on your loan approval!" They may not want everybody to know about their home purchase, so simply say "Congratulations!" It's up to them to share. Obviously if you sent your business cards they're able to share them with coworkers.

Here's a tip. Only deliver something that must be shared. If you send or take cook ies or cupcakes, that doesn't work. What will happen if you take cupcakes is they might have one for themselves and then put the rest of them under their desk to take home to their family. And no one else in their office is going to know they had an occasion to celebrate or that you are magnificent! You want to send something that makes a statement AND that they put in the kitchen, break, or conference room so that lots of people see it and wonder "What's going on?"

Perhaps you aren't comfortable taking a cake. I get that. Other ideas-and I'm sure you can come up with more-are pizza, balloons with candy, or a three-foot or longer sub sandwich with all the fixings. I would just encourage you to find something that you can take to your client that makes a huge impact.

I'm to the point where I'm not making the delivery myself. Rather, I reach out to a networking partner such as a cake decorator or a bakery and I have the cake delivered. It costs me a little bit more; the delivery charge is about $25. You can also hire a teenager or a mom who needs to make extra income while her kids are at school.

Remember, It's A Big Deal to Them

You can do so many different things to get noticed. The key is to make a big impact from a loan approval and not just send a quick email or make a phone call. I promise you, your client will be on the phone with you immediately, saying "Oh my gosh, I got the cake, it's so wonderful." And they will be so appreciative when you strategically show up personally to share the moment with them.

You know, I think we tend to get a little jaded about the importance of each indi vidual loan we handle. No matter how many loans you do in a month-it could be 5, 15, or 30-we tend to view any approval as just another approval, and we move on. But for the borrower it can be a really big deal. You should treat it as such.

Jen's Jots

♦ Stopping by your borrower's workplace to deliver an approval and con gratulations gift can be a fantastic way to deepen your relationship with the client and to spread the word about your practice.

♦ Bring a large cake or other edible gift that they can share with their coworkers.

♦ Be sure to include plenty of your business cards.

✳ Row, Row, Row the Boat

> **The Big Idea:** Approach referral partnerships with astrategic view on how you can help one another.
>
> *"First ..Give value, without expectation."*
>
> *- Jeffrey Gitomer*

A referral partner is anyone who can provide you a lead to a prospective client or a connection to someone who can help your business move forward. Let me emphasize how important it is to have robust and richrelationships with a variety of referral partners,

Why row a boat by yourself? You'll end up going in cirdes. Row withyour partners so you can both achieve success!

I truly believe that the foundation of my success in this business has been my abil ity to create collaborative, strategic partnerships, In this business, other people are so important to success, That's why I spend most of my days with, well other people! Referral partners deliver results that you can't replicate in any other way in your mortgage practice, Partnerships will:

♦ Enrich your life,

♦ Expand your access to prospects,

♦ Increase your market exposure,

♦ Help you give back,

♦ Give you a wide web of "team" members, and

♦ Offer cost-sharing opportunities,

A successful relationship with a referral partner is based on mutual trust and understanding of each other's business and business needs, and on educating each other on the kind of business you want, how to refer each other, setting expectations for clients as to what a partner expects or what you expect,reciproc ity, and lastly how to expand and expose one another in the marketplace.

In our business, real estate agents are our principal partners; however, if you are new to the business or have been in the business only a few years, most of your focus on building partnerships will be aimed at real estate agents for the time being. There is a wide world of potential referral partners available to help culti vate the expansion of your practice.

Looking at Partnerships inTermsof Client Readiness

Despite what I just said aboutthere being a huge world of potential referral part ners, all partners are not created equal. The referrals that any particular type of partner directs your way can be classified bestby how soon a client is to purchase a home and use your services. Understand then that a particular type of partner will generally refer a particular category of client on the readiness scale.

Let's look atthe accompanying table, "The Five Stages of Client Readiness."

Jennifer Du Plessis, CMPS, CME, COLS
Best Referral Sources
What makes a good Client or Connection for Jen?

HOT This referral is my Golden Goose. They're ready to Purchase or Refinance now!

- **Purdlaser** (If already working with lender? Ask them if they want a second opinion). These referrals are in need of being "Pre-Approved" or readyto buy but don't know how much they canafford.

- Refinance (These need someone to Manage their Mortgage OR they are interested in refinancing right now.

  CONNECTIONS: Realtors are my *Golden Geese,* Financial Advisors, Estate Planners

VERY WARM These referrals are a step down from Hot in that they might be ready in a month or tuvo...not immediate, but soon.

- Someone whose house is currently on the market to sell or thinking of selling

- Engaged to be married

- Considering refinancing but haven't looked intoit yet

  CONNECTIONS: Divorce Attorneys, Loan Officers at other Lenders, Real Estatelnvestors, Small Builders (5-20 homes built per year)

WARM A Warm referral is someone who is in need of my services but may not be ready for a while.

♦ Just started thinking about buying a first home or moving to a larger home.

♦ They may be currently renting and have 6-12 months left on their lease.

♦ They have had some credit issues in the past 2-3 years and need some one to guide them to fine tune their financial picture now, for the future.

♦ College bound children now or in the next few years for downsizing and/ or Kiddie Property purchase.

♦ Self employed for less than 2 years

CONNECTIONS: Tax Advisors, Insurance Agents (Life, Property, etc.)

LUKE WARM Luke warm referrals are those that mightneed my help sooner rather than later; even though they won't be obtaining a loan for some time.

♦ Perhaps mentioned they'd like to own a home of their own while in passing

♦ Are in the middle of a separation and/or divorce and some financial decisions need my expertise to resolve

♦ Upside down on their current home and need advice.

CONNECTIONS: Home Services Providers (HVAC, Handymen, Painters, Contractors)

TEPID This referral is a long shot and honestly they're just not ready right now; but we want to guide them for a future purchase in the coming years.

♦ This is a client who just declared bankruptcy, foreclosure or short sale.

♦ Credit issues are very bad and they have given up hope.

NOTE: These are broad introductions; but in the right hands, can be moved up the referral scale. This is annuity income for me.

CONNECTIONS: Miscellaneous Services (Travel, doctors, marketing, health care, etc)

REMEMBER: ALL OF THESE PEOPLE CAN REFER AS WELL.

Clients who are in any one of the five stages might be referred to you. The closer they are to Stage 5, the closer they are to making a purchase or refinance decision and needing your services.

No mortgage loan officer in the world receives 100 percent of their referrals at Stage 5; that is, clients who are always ready to buy now. However, understanding which referral partners generally refer clients in which stage enables you to view your relationships with these partners strategically. You will always need a steady stream of prospects that are in Stage 4 or Stage 5-that's a given. You also know that working with clients who are in Stage 2 or 3 means that they are a connection that you must nurture until they're ready to buy. Knowing this, you then can see what types of referral partners you need to cultivate in order to get connected to clients at all five levels of readiness. This view can help you if you have some glaring holes in your buyer readiness ladder.

In the remainder of this chapter, I want to discuss important aspects of strategic collaboration with the principal types of referral partners.

Financial Sector Partners

As you progress in your practice, I believe you'll come to see financial sector partners as equally important as real estate agent partners, if not more important.

As a member of the financial services sector of business, it makes sense that you focus your time and activities with other people in the same sector. Professionals in the financial arena include Certified Financial Planners (CFPs), financial advisors, estate planners, CPAs, tax advisors, attorneys, divorce attorneys, even mediators. Referrals from attorneys, financial planners, CPAs, and other financial services sector professionals are not reliant on the rise and fall of interest rates and other trends in the real estate market. People are always going through life changes such as marriage, birth of a child, an inheritance, divorce, a death , and kids leaving home. Financial services professionals are usually somewhere in the picture as these changes unfold. Who better to rub shoulders with in order to meet potential clients and help those clients with their mortgage needs?

Partnerships with financial professionals can be particularly strong and successful because these partnerships are:

♦ **Collaborative-You** and your partners are sharing in this venture, working as a team for the benefit of the client.

♦ **Strategic-Financial** professionals seek out strategies for growth and ways to improve communication and referral efforts as well as the long-term financial preparedness for clients' needs.

♦ **A Team Effort-Your** mutual reliance on each other is more important than any single client. They are your lifeline to not becoming a "mortgage commodity."

The best part of collaborating with financial professionals is that you now have a sales team of advocates "bird dogging" for you every day. And they know you are doing the same for them. If you've never worked with attorneys or financial advisors as referral partners, you'll find that they speak your language and are open to learning about ways to better serve their clients.

Successful Partnerships with Real Estate Agents

As I said a little earlier, real estate agents are the number one referral source for most loan officers. This is particularly true if you're new to the industry or have only been in the industry a couple of years.

For clients who are in the highest stage of buying readiness, Stage 5, it is generally going to be real estate agents who are referring these clients to you. They are the ones who are in contact with a potential client who is ready to strike now. They are partners who have clients who need a loan *today*.

Since all loan officers know that real estate agents are our "golden goose," we consequently pursue real estate agents relentlessly for business. In the next chapter we'll discuss how you, as a loan officer, can trigger the law of reciprocity with agents. That is, how you can be more in control of referrals by directing clients *TO* them, so that they then are motivated to direct clients *BACK* to you.

In your partnerships with real estate agents, it's important to consider altering your point of view. Instead of the thought 'What's in It *for* Me;" think "What's in It *from* Me?" Ask yourself: What can you give to your partners that will improve their business or personal situation? We all know this, we just have to remember to think of it because when we give, we will in turn receive.

The "What's in It *from* Me" attitude also extends to the level of customer service and value you deliver to real estate agents. Differentiating yourself via value added thinking will absolutely guarantee repeat business.

What do real estate agents see as value-added services from loan officers? I asked one of the most successful real estate agents in the Washington, D.C. area what she wants to experience when working with a loan officer, and here are a few of her suggestions for building a successful, long-term relationship. She said a loan officer should:

◆ Help educate the buyer about the purchase and loan process. Add value to the agent's services by educating the client so the agent doesn't have to.

◆ Help set client expectations. Tell them what to expect, why, and when.

◆ Keep the client and the agent up to date and in the loop so that there are no client questions and concerns about the loan process that land in the agent's lap unexpectedly.

◆ Be in control of the process. Communicate with the client and agent simultaneously on any and all developments, concerns, documentation needs, schedules, etc.

◆ Take responsibility. If there is a stumble or problem in the loan process and it is zero percent your fault, own it anyway. Communicate immediately with the agent and figure out a solution.

♦ Close on Time, every time.

♦ Look for ways to help each other. You are in the industry to help people, so make the whole process easier and more satisfying by helping each other help the client.

♦ Spark opportunities to cross promote and to expand and expose your business.

The Very Broad Regular Category of Partner

If you partner only with real estate agents and financial services professionals, I have no doubt that you will have a successful practice. However, partnering with a wide range of other service providers can lead to referrals that will also pay off handsomely over the long term. They can be plumbers, electricians, home improvement contractors, handymen, maid services, landscapers, carpet clean ers, hair dressers, doctors, and really anyone connected with both homeowners and renters.

Anybody you talk to can be a referral partner, but there can be a lot of variation in the quality of a referral from a given partner. In general, referrals from home services providers will be of clients who are in Stage 1, 2, or 3 of buying readiness, That is, they can be several years away from applying for a home loan.

Partners such as CPAs, attorneys, and insurance agents usually provide referrals to clients in buying readiness stages 2 to 4.

Having a range of clients in your database will contribute to the long-term growth of your practice. As far as I'm concerned, I want to meet everybody who may at some point need my services. It might be that they're two years or three years away from buying a home and needing a mortgage-that's okay. It's up to me to communicate with them, to nurture them along to the point where they will need a loan. So I want the connection as soon as possible.

The goal isn't for me to do a loan for them this month or this year. The goal is to keep in touch with them and stay top of mind while they're moving up from Stage 1 or 2 to Stage 5.

The key to getting referrals from other service providers is to educate these pro viders on how to refer you and when to recognize an opportunity to refer you.

For example, while working in a client's home, they may have oppo rtun iti es to hear about a client's goals, plans, and wishes. It can be something as innocuous as "Boy, our house is feeling kind of cramped these days." If you've educated your partner to recogniz e the se typ es of trigg er stat eme nts as a pot ential referral op portunity , the service provider can ask if the client would like to be connected to you.

As I said, these kinds of referrals offer you built-in, long-term business growth. They put medium-term and long-term prospects into your pipeline. You can work these clients up the ladder of readiness.

The Know, Like, and Trust Equation

The bottom line for any referral partnership is to be fruitful: a partner has to know, like, and trust you. That's simply a basic premise of sales!

Therein lies one of the biggest issues with loan officers, in my view. The typical loan officer "sells" themselves to a prospective partner in a shallow way. "Hey, I'm a loan officer! You should know what I do, so send some business my way!" But you'll never have any success with that attitude. A partner may know <u>what</u> you do but not <u>who</u> you are. Until that time, they can't possibly grow to like you and subsequently trust you. Therefore, they're highly unlikely to refer a client to you.

You have to take the time and make the effort to learn about a partner's practice and to educate them about yours. You have to put in the time and effort to get to really know them personally and professionally, and to understand their busi ness goals. Then you can work with them from a place of abundance rather than scarcity.

Again, it goes back to my slightly altered definition ofWIIFM. Always think, What's in It *from* Me? What can I give to this partner? How can I help their business? How can I enrich their lives? When you give to partners-be it through value, cross promotion or increased exposure, or referrals-they will give back to you.

I hope this alters your perception about your relationship with referral partners. Always look for ways to give-it will make an incredible difference in your practice.

Jen's Jots

♦ Never forget: Referral partners are the foundation of your success in the mortgage industry.

♦ Think strategically about the kinds of partners you need to cultivate according to the buying readiness of the clients they refer.

♦ Build robust relationships with the three principal types of partners: real estate agents, financial services professionals, and home services provid ers.

Stage 5: Hot. They are ready to purchase or refinance NOW.

♦ Purchaser: Clients in need of being "pre-approved" or ready to buy but don't know how much they can afford; or purchaser already working with a lender and perhaps is in need of a "second opinion."

♦ Refinance: Clients who need someone to manage their mortgage or they are inter ested in refinancing right now.

♦ Prime Partners: Real estate agents, financial advisors, small builders (5 to 20 homes built per year).

Stage 4: Very Warm. Clients a step down from hot. May be ready in a month or two; not an immediate need, but soon.

♦ Someone thinking of selling current home.

♦ Someone whose house is currently on the market, but no offers in hand.

♦ A couple engaged to be married.

♦ Considering refinancing but haven't looked into it yet.

Prime Partners: Divorce attorneys, loan officers at other lenders, real estate inves tors, estate planners.

Stage 3: Warm. Someone who may need your services but may not be ready fora while.

♦ Have just started thinking about buying a first home or moving to a larger home.

♦ May be currently renting and have 6 to 12 months left on their lease.

♦ May have had some credit issues in the past two to three years and need someone to guide them to fine tune their financial picture for the future.

♦ College bound children now or in the next few years looking at downsizing, or looking at helping children purchase a home.

♦ Self-employed for less than two years.

Prime Partners: Tax advisors, insurance agents (life, property, etc ....)

Stage 2: Lukewarm. Potential clients that *might* need your help sooner rather than later, even though they won't be obtaining a loanfor sometime.

♦ Perhaps mentioned in passing they'd like to own a home of their own.

♦ Are in the middle of a separation and/or divorce and need your expertise on some financial decisions.

♦ Upside down on their current home and need advice.

Prime Partners: Home services providers (HVAC,handymen, painters, contractors)

Stage1:Tepid.Areferral that Isalong shot,and honestly they'l'eJust not ready or ablerightnow,*bur* **you wanttoguldethemfor atuturepurchase** In **thecoming years.**

♦   Someone who just declared bankruptcy, or went through a foreclosure or short sale.

♦   Their credit issues are <u>*very*</u> bad and they have given up hope.

♦   These are broad introductions, but in the right hands can be moved up the referral scale. Can be viewed as annuity income.

Prime Partners: Miscellaneous services (travel, doctors, marketing, health care, etc.)

Remember: Anyone, in any stage, can be a greatsource to refer friends, family, coworkers, etc., as well!

✳ Differentiate Yourself by Being an Educator

The Big Idea: *Create value for your partners and differentiate yourself by conducting and sponsoring educational seminars, classes, and other events,*

"The biggest room in the world is the room for improvement"

- Harvey MacKay

Being a business builder rather than a business beggar is about differentiating yourself from other loan officers and about providing value to your partners. A terrific way to accomplish those goals is to deliver presentations, seminars, and classes that help partners with their businesses. You'll become a recognized expert and the "go-to" loan officer.

Now, this is my opinion, but I think many people in the mortgage industry spend a tremendous amount of energy and money on things that don't give them any traction. One example might be open houses and broker opens. Be honest with yourself: is that real estate agent who asks you to co-sponsor something with them really going to give you any business? If you find that you're beating your head against the wall and you're doing a lot of these broker opens and you're just not getting the results, then I would just ask you to think: Am I really giving value to this real estate agent, or am I just giving them money? I recognize that you may be reading this and find open houses and broker opens valuable, so please keep doing them.

I decided a long time ago-and it's partly why I teach and educate people-that I wasn't going to be like everybody else and do all the typical loan officer activities. In fact, I can probably count on two hands the number of broker opens that I have done in my entire career-in over 30 years. I just don't want to be used, quite frankly, and I know that you don't want to be used either.

What I decided was that I was going to be the educator and the subject matter expert. I decided to be the person who delivered *value* to real estate agents through Eduselling: educating and selling at the same time.

Presentations

Lot's talk first about presentations. What I mean here is presentations in real estate offices. Now I'm quite aware that there are a lot of closed offices, but it's not as difficult as you may think to work with those offices that are receptive.

If you have the opportunity to do a presentation at a real estate office, I think that's wonderful. I don't do as many of those anymore, but when I do they are not product specific, and they are not info-dumping commercials about our rates, products, and customer service. They are about providing valuable education to help the agents in their businesses.

During a presentation, you just want to give agents the sizzle, not the steak. You give them ideas and ways that you can help them in their business. You're trying to compel them to want to meet with you, so for example you might want to do a presentation on how to hold a successful home buyers' seminar. If they have interest in doing one, they can follow up with you afterwards on how to put that together.

I often talk to my top referral partners separately to coordinate seminars and classes that we hold as a team.

Seminars

I'm a seminar junkie. I go to them and I hold them. Anytime there's a seminar or a class being offered for real estate agents, I urge you to attend it and be one of the attendees in the classroom and learning. I feel that anything we can learn, any of these classes that we attend, even if it might be about real estate ethics or contract writing, we are going to learn something that will help us in our business because it will help us relate to the agents.

Additionally, you're now a student in the same class. It's great to be able to spend some quality time with potential partners. I can tell you that as a speaker you don't have the same opportunity to meet with all the people that are attending your class. You don't because when there's a break or the seminar is over, there will be two or three attendees who will ask you questions, holding you hostage. The others will see there's a line and they will decide to leave. So, as an attendee you will have more opportunities to chat with people.

What about teaching a seminar? What about holding a regular weekly or monthly session for agents as a series on how they can improve their business? Perhaps hold a 10-week lunch-and-learn every Wednesday at noon. That is a perfect way for you to get several real estate agents to attend from a variety of offices. Be sure to bring your referral partners, too, because they want to meet agents and this is a great opportunity for them.

Currently, I have 26 hours of continuing education (CE) courses approved to teach to both realtors and financial advisors.

I always have a seminar or a class scheduled, always something going on. Here are a couple of examples of what I typically have scheduled. One thing I often do is a home buyer's seminar with a real estate agent; in fact, we've turned this into a series. The reason I like to do a series is because with a one-time seminar you sometimes end up having more speakers than attendees. The reason that hap pens is if you only offer it once, people will intend to come or want to come but can't for some reason on the one day you're holding the seminar.

If you have a series it allows you to provide the same information in smaller sec tions so that people can come to different parts of the series. It also allows you to give your attendees evaluations or survey forms to find out what other topics they want to hear about so you can add these into your series or extend your series. Additionally, it gives them the opportunity to attend and be so inspired and wowed that they tell their friends and their friends start showing up at your next session in the series.

A series gives you consistent opportunities to market. Let's say you hold a series the third Thursday of every month or the second Wednesday of every month. You can always be marketing these events. You can include them in your email signature and do a link to Google calendar and show all the events that you have planned, you can place it on Facebook and post the schedule on your Facebook page, and you can do an Evite invitation. Pretty soon people will know that you have a seminar series on a regular basis.

This is particularly important with your real estate agent partners, because now that they know you hold a seminar on a regular basis they can consistently invite their home buyers to an ongoing seminar to keep their prospects engaged as well.

Conducting home seller's se minars is another option. Just as there are first-time home buyers, there are first-time home sellers. They don't know exactly what to expect, much like they didn't know what to expect when they were buying the home. So, for a first-time ho me seller seminar you might have a home stager or home inspector who gives them tips on what improvements to make on their home. And certainly, you can hold this type of seminar in conjunction with your real estate agents as well, especially listing agents. I've asked, "Who of your past clients were first-time home buyers and now might be thinking about selling in the next year or so? Le t's get them in now and start educating them with a first-time seller seminar."This has provided me another gr eat av enu e of refe rrals.

Another seminar series that I've held over the years is a Re al Estate Mortgage Finance (math) class. They absolut ely love it. It began as a three-hou r session, and is now two three-hour sessions. I now offer Math 101 and Math 201 seminars and have obtained approval for 6 hours of continuing education for Realtors ®.

Any more when I teach a class or do a presentatio n, I strategically pick and choose the real estate agents that I might want to approach as a prospective partner. When you first begin teaching it will provide you with opportunities to meet as many agents as you wish. Later, you will become more selective and only approach a handful with whom you might consider having a profitable business relationship.

Be Creative, Deliver Value

You can conduct lunch-and-learns, hold evening events, or even sponsor busi ness mixers. I sponsor a business mixer once a quarter. I invite all my top referral partners and real estate agents to the same mixer so I can be the connector for their business expansion. It's also great to be able to introduce agents to one another, because there may be an occasion in the future when they might be involved in a transaction. I hold mixers at a local restaurant/bar. You can charge a nominal fee for a mixer, which goes toward appetizers, and you can usually nego tiate some reduced drink prices. At the mixers I sponsor, I usually attract between 30 and 50 attendees. Don't forget to engage with another partner to co-sponsor!

Another option for gathering partners or prospects together is to hold a client party. It's a great way for you to introduce clients to referral partners. Be sure to have your referral partners speak for a few minutes.

I've also done something I call wine and wisdom. I've done Wealthy, Healthy, and Wise as well. There are all different kinds of events you can do, but wine and wisdom is an event for either just your real estate partners, your clients, or your generic partners. They have a little wine and they get a little wisdom -not from me, but from someone else that might be beneficial to them. So, for example, with wine and wisdom with real estate agents I have had a credit company talk about credit repair. The funny thing about that is that most of the agents need their own credit repair, so they loved it. The purpose is just to share with them how they could help clients get credit repair.

I've had an HVAC person who talked about why, in a house, it can be cold in one room and hot in another, and about things that agents can look for as they're walking through a home with a buyer. I've had an insurance agent come in and talk about whether agents are carrying enough insurance. You know, agents may face potential liabilities they don't think about, such as using their own vehicles to drive clients around, so the insurance agent spoke to them about how to protect themselves.

My message to you is to think of ways to *deliver value.* Seminars and presenta tions are a constant in my practice. In any given month, I may have anywhere from two to four scheduled events and/or teaching opportunities.

You want to dominate your market as THE educator. I can honestly tell you I can walk into a real estate association happy hour or event and people will approach me and say, "Oh my gosh, I attended your class two years ago. I thank you so much for your class. When is your next class scheduled?" And these are real estate agents that I've not yet connected with.

So get out there. Create value, help people in their busine sses, and business will come your way.

Jen's Jots

♦ Develop educational events for your partners, help them with their busi ness, and help them serve their clients better.

♦ When you create value for your partners, you differentiate yourself in the market and give yourself an edge over your competition.

♦ Don't forget about your clients. Evening and weekend events that build your community or educate them for their next life-event work great.

✳ Dig Deeper with this Technique

> **The Big Idea:** *Get to know a partner or a client on a deeper level by using the FROG conversation starter technique.*
>
> *"Arrogance is deadly."*
>
> *-Anonymous*

Let's dig deeper into how to conduct a quality and profitable business meeting with your clients and referral partners to build richer relationships and to assess their needs on an on-going basis.

Delving deeper into a partner's or client's background will open doors to find commonality. It will also prevent you from talking too much about yourself rather than talking more about them. You can demonstrate to clients that they're not just a number or another person who's put on the conveyor belt we call the loan process. You'll be able to find ways to move away from the mundane efficiency of a transaction into creating a great customer experience for your clients AND your referral partners.

I want to discuss an important way to discover more about the people you come into contact with, soyou can be more in tune with their needs. There are other methods I use, such as assessing the needs of your clients through mortgage planning questionnaires, but for now, let's start with one of my favorite things: acronyms!

Get to Know Someone Using"FROG"

Have you ever heard of using FROG or FORD as a way to trigger ideas on how to get to know someone? FROG stands for Family, Recreation, Occupation, and Goals. FORD is basically the same technique, butthe acronym represents Family, Occupation, Recreation, and Dreams. Either one works wonders.

When you're meeting with a client, or a referral partner, if you cankeep the FROG system in the forefront of your mind, it will always prevent you from talking too much aboutyourself rather than learning more aboutthem. For example, for the F, you might ask them about their Family; their children, their birthdays, where they went to school/college,what sports they like, or how long they've been married andwhat they do to celebrate their wedding anniversary. You might just ask them what they like to do with their family for fun.

In any case, your interest is really setting you up for some great relationship development ideas. So while you have a systematic process for being able to push a loanthrough and it's very transactional on the operations side,you wantto be able to project to the client that they're getting a unique experience from you. They're not just a number or another faceless person on this conveyor belt. That's where asking them about their family comes in. You might even be pleasantly surprised to find out that they have other family members who you could help.

When asking about the R for recreation, whatI do is usually say,"What do you like to do for fun? What's out there for you when you're not working and you're not spending time withyour family?"

Asking questions such as these will open up some doors to find some commonal ity, not just between you and the client or partner, but also involving members of your team. This becomes important when you have a team or you have other people in your practice who are communicating with the borrower. So, for exam ple, if someone said, 'Well, you know, I really love wakeboarding," and wouldn't you know it, you've got a processor or someone else on your team who will be communicating with the borrower who is a wakeboarder as well. This gives you a perfect opportunity to communicate and relay that information to other parties on your team so that when they have conversations with the client, they can say, "Oh gosh, I hear you love wakeboarding. I do, too. Where do you go? How long have you been doing it?"

This allows us to move away from the mundane efficiency of a transaction into creating a great customer experience for our clients AND for our referral partners. Can you imagine if your assistant who's writing the preapproval letter for a new real estate agent sends the letter over and says, "'Oh, by the way,I understand that you're a huge wine connoisseur. I'm from California and I love wine, too, I can't wait to talk to you about it." These little things really go a long way;take mental, written, or audio notes of what you hear that could be utilized to form stronger relationships and connections.

Of course, asking about someone's Occupation comes naturally. You can ask,"Tell me what you do and who do you seNe?" or "Why did you get into this particular business?" Again, these work whether you're talking with a client or a referral partner. "'So, why did you decide to become a real estate agent? What compelled you to be a financial planner? What was your degree in that brought you to this point? What does the future look like for you?" These are great opportunities to talk about their occupation and what their passion is. Really dig deep to find the passion so thatyou can highlight thatwhen you're meeting with them on a regular basis and over time as you're developing that relationship.

The lastpart of the acronym stands for Goals, and of course in FORD, it's dreams. Perhaps you could ask, "What do you want to achieve with what you're doing in this line of work? How many clients do you want to have? What do you envision for your growth in the next few years? What does it look like for you, and when you're done with this business and this industry, what does that look like? What do you plan to do?"

Again, this technique works great with your clients. If you're taking an application, you will obviously be asking about their job. But what if you just stopped for a moment-move away from being an order-taker-and asked them, "Wow, that's really interesting. What got you into that? Where's your passion?"

Exploring and learning more information is very easy to do. This technique is very easy-if youremember to do it! It demonstrates and shows people that you care about them. It comes from a servant heart, and I hope you're the type of person who has a servant heart, too. So hopefully you'll naturally use the FROG process in the needs analysis so you can really identify the needs of your clients.

Hint: For Heaven's sake, please don't talk with someone and ask a series of ques tions from F to G. This is conversational. In fact, you may not get to all of the let ters in one meeting.

When working with clients, you might want to ask, "What might your world look like after you have been in this house five years from now?" You should discuss with them an entrance strategy, a maintenance strategy, and then an exit strategy out of this home and out of this mortgage. What goals do they have? Do they want their mortgage to create wealth for them through equity? Do they want their mortgage to provide them with a better cash flow so that they can divert the funds into savings and for college and for retirement? Assess the goals of the client and really spend some time getting to know theirs.

Make Conversation Easier

I know from many of my conversations, and especially with my coaching clients, there are so many people who are afraid to pick up the phone, or afraid to have a meeting with a real estate agent more than one time. Using the FROG technique makes the conversation flow more comfortable for everyone .

Now you are talking about business and it gives you a reason to have the next meeting. A suggestion to keep the conversation moving along and engaging is to book the next lunch right there on the spot. Then you won 't have to make phone calls to ask, "Hey, do you want to go to lunch? Do you want to grab a coffee?" Instead the phone call is just, "Hello, I'm just confirming that we're meeting." This eliminates some of the fear of making the follow-up phone call. I would hate for you to have done all the work to make a connection, finally get a meeting, only to have met once and then you're done. You cert ainly won't be able to establish any relationships just meeting people once.

Keep employing these conversations so you're able to have fresh content and topics of discussions when meeting people to develop stronger, deeper, and richer relationships; be able to assess their needs; and then cultivate effective ways to become strategic partners.

Jen's Jots

♦ Use the FROG conversation starter technique to get to know your partners and clients. Ask about their:

- ♦ F-Family
- ♦ R-Recreation
- ♦ 0-Occupation
- ♦ G-Goals

✳ Three Quick Questions to Get In-Depth Perspective

> **The Big Idea:** Develop a deeper understanding of a referral partner's practice by asking these three simple questions about the past, future, and present
>
> *"Watch your attitude. It's the first thing people notice about you."*
>
> *-Anonymous*

With any referral partner, you want to know how their practice best fits with your practice. The question is, how do you get to this understanding? Obviously, you need to have one-on-one meetings with them to learn about how they do business.

Just a quick get-together with typical business small talk won't get you to a broader and in-depth perspective. For that, you need to dive deeper. Let me give you a great way to develop richer relationships with a referral partner, whether they are a real estate agent, financial planner, or plumber.

The first way is to ask them about three past, three future, and three present clients, That is, ask them about the three most recent clients they've worked with, three clients they'll be working with in the near future, and three clients they're working with now. Getting into a detailed discussion based on these three ques tions will give you exceptionally useful and valuable information about the part ner's business,

Three Past Clients

Remember Chapter 4-16? Who your partners are working with may define the types of referrals you receive and how quickly you may be able to close a loan, Questions about past, future, and present clients help you pinpoint the types of clients a partner typically works with-obviously, this has important implications for who the partner might refer to you.

The first question is about the past: Ask the partner about the last three clients they've worked with. Therefore, for a realtor that could be a listing, a buyer, a renter, an investor-it could be a range of client types, Then go a little deeper in the conversation by asking some probing follow-up questions. What did you do for them? How did you feel when you were helping them? Who did you get the referral from?How did you get that client? If a recent client was a repeat customer, for example, you can use thatknowledge when you're talking to clients and refer ring them to this agent. You can let your clients know that this agent has repeat business, which says a lot about their service. A partner's answer to the question about where a recent pastreferral came from can be revealing.

With this line of questioning, you can get a sense of who the partner has been working with and whattheir clients are like. This can provide some insight on how the two of you can work together. You really get some great perceptions into who these people are, how they feel about their business, and what's important to them about working with clients.

Now by the way, if you want to ask about just one past client instead of three, that's fine.However,I find that three is better because it givesme a more rounded view of their business than does asking aboutjust one past client. You could also use this as a strategy to have multiple meetings to uncover other past clients.

Next,theFuture Clients

Who are the next three people you're meeting with? Are they listing appoint ments? Are they rentals? Are they just lookie-lous, first-time, Millennials, or down sizing buyers? Or maybe it's another referral partner? Be sure to ask them how these clients were referred or how they met.

They maytell you they're going to be meeting with a buyer. You can ask how they met the buyer, what the buyer is looking for, and what their challenges might be, while all the time you're collecting and filing away information to possibly to ask for business or a connection.

Now,thePresent Clients

The question you can ask here is: "Who are you working with right now?" You always want to know how they're generating their business; you always want to dig deeper into their world. You want to know how and where they get their busi ness so you can possibly co-brand with them and co-network and co-refer and work together. If they're in the midst of a buying process with a client,you can ask if they're working with a lender and,if so,why they chose that lender. You wantto gain great intelligence into how they decide which lender to work with.

Now, they might respond that the lender gave the buyer to them. You probably don't want to hear that because most lenders don't do that, but occasionally you will hear that. But it does offer some insight into the fact that other lenders are getting leads and passing them on to realtors. So, you better start working on ways you can do that as well. You will also gain insight into what they like about the lender so you can perhaps add an action, event, or communication tool to your process.

They might tell you that they've either worked with that lender forever or just began working with them. This is a crossroads in finding out about their business. You can ask if they work with any other lenders, or you can ask if they're open to a new relationship. This can also be a perfect time to ask if they have a need for a second opinion or if a double application would be helpful. Asking about the present opens immediate opportunities for business today.

Reciprocate and Keep Moving Deeper

I don't have the space to give you every angle for every situation. You simply should ask simple questions that center on their business and what's happening in their practice on a daily and weekly basis. It helps you understand their practice. Be curious. Then you can find an angle that you can use to either obtain a referral, get an introduction to a new connection, or know how best to provide your services and products.

When you show interest in someone else, they're naturally going to ask you the same questions so that they understand what kind of business you do as well. Always be prepared to answer the questions as well so you don't lose an opportunity to expand your business too.

It's natural for them to ask you and reciprocate. If they don't ask, do not hesitate to say, "Thank you so much for sharing, wow, that really gives me some insight into where your business comes from, how you operate, and I would love the opportunity to share with you the same things about my practice." You may or may not be able to do it at that same meeting, so if you're able to, great, run with it. If you're not able to, go ahead and schedule your next appointment.

Schedule your next meeting while the two of you are still together and have your calendars in front of you. That will keep the partnership momentum going.

BONUS: A colleague of mine, Michael Griffiths, the Referral Guru, shared with me his powerful program for working with referral partners. He taught three other questions (with some "Jen style" mixed in) that I have used for years to gain richer relationships with my partners.

Every time I have a scheduled face-to-face or phone meeting with a partner I will use these three questions:

◆　Tell me about one of your goals this week/month and how I can help support you in achieving it? You now become their accountability partner, whether the goal is business or personal.

◆ Who would you like to be connected with this week/month to help expand your business? This cannot be answered with "any buyer." It can be a specific *type* of buyer, such as someone who just became engaged. But, more specifically, this question is directed toward someone they would like to meet to create another collaborative relationship.

◆ What <u>specifically</u> can I do for you this week/month? Again, this is not "a buyer" or lead. Perhaps your partner is holding a client appreciation party, grand opening, or open house. Maybe they are looking for a new hire and need your help to spread the word. Or perhaps they have a huge deadline and simply need your moral support.

The goal of these three questions is to help one another expand and explore your respective practices. After you use them, they can now ask you the same ques tions, so be prepared. I hold weekly and monthly call and meetings with a handful of my partners, and we review these three questions each time.

Jen's Jots

◆ In order to gain a deeper and richer understanding of a partner's business practices and how you can best work with them, ask them about their three past, future, and present clients.

◆ Ask some probing follow-up questions that will give you insight into how they do business.

If you haven't used this technique before and you need to ease into it, at your next several partner one-on-ones, ask about their 2 past, 2 present, and 2 future clients, or even 1-1-1.

✳ What's In a Name?

> **The Big Idea:** *Train your referral partners on how to describe you when they refer someone. This is crucial for your branding and image.*
>
> *"We must all suffer from one of two pains: the pain of discipline or the pain of regret. The difference is discipline weighs ounces while regret weighs tons."*
>
> *-JimRohn*

One key aspect of being referred by a partner and referring a partner to someone is the words you use to describe each other. It's not something you should leave to chance-it canbe very important to your brand and image.

Think about this. If you leave it up to partners to figure out how to describe you, they'll be defining your brand. The problem is, if every partner says something a little different about you, you really have no brand. And the reverse is also true: the brand and image of a partner is defined as soon as you describe them to a client.

I protect my brand by training my referral partners on what they should say about me when they refer me. I think educating my partners in this way is really crucial. What I don't want someone to say is, "Call Jen. She's a mortgage broker I work with." I don'twant to be called a mortgage broker. I don't wantto be called a loan officer. I want to be referred to as a Certified Mortgage Planner.

So it's really important to me that I educate and train my referral partners on how I want to be referred. I find the best way to do that is to write my own mini-bio or suggested introduction, based on who they are and the potential clients they will generally refer.

For example, the description I give to a financial planner will be more sophisti cated than the description I give to a plumber. For the financial planner, I'm going to use more financial terms in my description, such as,"Jen is a discerning expert in her field. She will guide you through the lending path and strategically align your goals and needs with the right mortgage for you. She will address your entrance strategy, your holding strategy, and what you planto do while you have the home, along with your exit strategy as well. During the time you have the home,she will manage your mortgage as a complementary service to ensure that you have timely updates about the market." The description will be more sophis ticated to resonate with a financial planner for their clients.

I'm not going to ask a plumber to describe me in that way. I'll ask a plumber to say something along the lines of, "Listen, I really trust Jen, she is a top national Certified Mortgage Planner, and I know she will take care of you because of the relationship she has with me," This is more plain-spoken.

With my generic referral partners, I educate them to ask the people they encoun ter "whether they own or rent?" If they rent, I educate the partner to tell the cli ent if they've ever thought about buying, that he or she works with a fantastic mortgage planner. That can be followed by an offer to introduce me because I can help get the client on the right path,whether they plan to buy soon or two to three years from now.

If they are a homeowner,I would like the partner to ask the client,"Oh,wellwho's managing your mortgage?" This is an entree to a referral to me to manage their mortgage. The answer to that question is typically, well,Wells Fargo or SunTrust or some bank that they're making their payments to. The servicer is not managing their mortgage-they are only collecting the payment. What I'm looking for is to have people think of me as Jen, the person who manages their mortgage, and not the company I represent.

My partner can say, "Listen, I know a wonderful college who is a Certified Mortgage Planner." (And I've educated and trained them to answer the ques tion of 'What's that? Is that more expensive than a loan officer, what are you talking about?" so they know how to respond.) But they can say, "She manages mortgages. She can provide you with timely updates on mortgage market trends, rates, and other valuable homeownership,wealth building content so you can be in-the-know rather than wonder."

The goal, of course, is to move these potential clients into my contact database and then give them updates and review their mortgage annually for them. This puts them into the queue possibly for me to work with them on their next pur chase, or refinance, or a referral to a friend, family member, or colleague. But this all hinges on having my partners educated and readyto ask the 'Who's managing your mortgage?" question when an opportunity arises.

Branding Your Partners

On the flip side, of course,I want my partners to educate me as to what I should say aboutthem.I typically ask my referral partners to write a mini-bio about them selves that I can use when I refer them.

I ask, 'What are the things thatyou would like me to say aboutyou?" This enables me to offer a cogent, well-thought out third-party evaluation of the partner. This doesn't need to be lengthy. When I'm referring that partner I can just copy and paste the description-perhaps with some moderate tweaks customized for the person I'm sending it to.

Keep your branding consistent. Make sure you educate your referral partners on what to say about you. Ask them to do the same so you're not saying something generic that doesn't maintain their brand as well.

Jen's Jots

♦ Give each particular type of partner a tailored description of your services that fits withtheir business and the type of client they will generally refer.

♦ Ask your referral partners to write a description of themselves and their services that you can use when you refer them.

✳ Match Maker

> **The Big Idea:** You can best serve your clients if you have partnership relationships with a spectrum of partners in the same field.
>
> "Thinking is the hardest work there is;
> probably why so few people engage in it."
>
> -Henry Ford

Yes,you can have multiple business partnerships with the same type of referral partner without harming any of your relationships. In fact, itisinthebest interests of serving your clients to have more than one partnership in any given area.

One of my coaching clients asked me recently if having too many financial plan ners in her database would dilute the relationship with any given partner.

The answer is, "No." What I've found is that as a loan officer,you have to have partnership relationships with several of the same type of provider-such asfinan cial planners-in order to cover the full spectrum of your client types and client preferences. Think of this on a scale or a kind of linear arrangement. On the left side of the scale, you have a financial planner who is willing to talk to a clientwho has absolutely no cash, but is interested in learning about budgeting and maybe just wants to start saving a few hundred dollars a month. On the other end of the spectrum, you mayhave a financial planner who won'twork with anyone who has anything less than $5 million in investable assets.

You want to cover the full spectrum of what a particular service provider does for a living and what type of clients they serve. The best way to carve that out is to ask a prospective partner where 80 percent of their business comes from. Again, using the example of financial planners, if 80 percent of a planner's business comes from people who make $100,000 a year, thenthat's the type of client you need to send to them, not higher-end clients.

That's the first aspect to having multiple partnerships.

The second aspect is having the ability to make a good match while taking into consideration personality, age dynamic,location,and the like.

Maybe you work with a financial planner who is 30years of age andyou also work with a financial planner who is 60 years of age,andyour client is 25. So you have to consider that on each side of the spectrum of financial planners you work with youmay need a relationship withtwo or three in the same space for purposes of matching by personality and age dynamic.

Location is also an important factor in larger metropolitan areas. For example, in the area I live and work in, metropolitan Washington, D.C., I could have a client who lives 80 miles west of the city and commutes into Washington, D.C. for their job. That's not out of the ordinary. So if I have a client who's 80 miles away from Washington, D.C., andthey commute into Washington, D.C. to work,it could make sense for them to work with a financial planner in the city during work hours. But it also might make sense for them to work with a financial planner who is located closer to where they live. It is in my best interest to have a relationship with a financial planner in both locations.

By having partner relationships with several providers in the same field you can precisely direct and refer your clients to best meet their needs.

Jen's.k>ts

- ◆ Cultivate referral relationships with multiple professionals and service pro viders in the same field.

- ◆ Multiple relationships offer you a full spectrum of partner capabilities for your clients.

- ◆ Introduce partners and clients according to how they match up in the mar ket space,their interpersonal and age dynamics, and location preference.

✳ Success Stories and Recommendations

> **The Big Idea:** What other people say about you is the most effective marketing tool you can have.
>
> "Nothing great can be achieved without enthusiasm."
>
> - Ralph Waldo Emerson

Prospective clients and referral partners want to have some proof that you're the ideal loan officer to work with. And they're not just going to take your word for it!

Just as in any marketing, the most powerful elementto convince someone to use your services or to work with you,is social proof-what other people say about you. That's why success stories and recommendations are so powerful. Let's talk in detail here about how to create success stories, get written recommendations, and then how to use these extremely powerful marketing tools.

We all have success stories we could share but we sometimes forget to write them down right away and then later we can't remember them. I want to encour age you to begin thinking about some of your success stories about the seNice you gave that made clients very happy. Perhaps at least once a month capture these success stories, and think through what you did to make the situation a success.

Maybe it was a client who had really bad credit and you worked with them for a year or two years and then they finally were able to get their home. How did you achieve loan success? How did the client feel before, during, and after the process? Utilize time during your monthly sales meeting to share success stories withyour team and processor. There may be storiesyou are not aware of.

Creating a centralized location where everyone can add letters, comments, or stories could be a time efficient way to manage your successes.

Using Success Stories

Let's talk about how to success stories in your practice.

One way I use them is during myreferral partner process-this being the 70 days after I've met with a potential new referral partner. I send a total of four success stories, one every other week over the course of two months. I do this to keep myself top of mind and to ensure they don't stereotype me into the same category as other loan officers. For example, I have one success story about a first-time homebuyer, one about a client that had a credit situation, and one about a client who relocated and how stressful it was for them and how happy they were at the end. I have another that really enhances my certified mortgage planning skills and about how I restructured a refinance.

You want to have a nice range of topics to share. When I choose what to share, I'm always mindful of what the partners does (their niche) and who they are so the subject matter is relevant. I repeat the same stories for all partners because I'm sending them right after I've had my first one-to-one with a new referral partner. While all stories are fresh and new for the m, they may be a duplicate for me.

Another way that I use success stories is that I share them with potential clients. Maybe a client has a situation similar to a past client. I want to make sure they know I'm capable of handling the situation for them.

Success stories are very valuable. You can use them with borrowers, real estate agents, referral partners, really anyone to whom you want to provide some social proof. My financial planner partners love seeing success stories-again, being mindful that they like to see stories describing how I would use mortgage strate gies in serving their client referrals. If you're trying to break in with financial plan ners or estate planners, use success stories.

If you're not confident in your writing abilities, by all means hire a competent freelance writer to writ e for you. They can probably come up with some interest ing angles you wouldn't think of. If you write the success stories yourse lf, to make it efficient and non-time consuming, follow a formula. Try this four-step process: describe the client's situation/background, cite the challenge they faced, describe the solution you developed, and summarize the results .

Generating and Using Client Recommendations

Your success in generating recommendation letters is tied directly to how you educate your clients about how you work by referral and your desire to receive referrals from them. They didn't go to "customer school" as our Chief experi ence Officer (CXO), Steve Dor fman, frequently alludes to, so most likely they are unaware that you are seeking their feedback.

Here's a suggestion. After receiving a stellar survey-assuming you ask for sur veys-you could take a few action steps. First, you could call the client and thank them for completing the survey. Ensure they are settled into their new home and check to confirm how everything's going and ask how they are enjoying their new home. Be sure to check to make sure they've received their first payment coupon or if they've received notification whether their servicing has been sold, and if they have any questions. Likely, they will compliment you again (as they did in the survey), creating a heightened state of gratitude. This is your opportunity to ask for the business-remember that you have earned the right to ask! Our CXO has taught our team to use this scripting: "Thank you so much for that, it made my day. This is why I do what I do; and you can say no to this, and you wouldn't hurt my feelings, but would you be willing, if I provided you with a link, to go onto Zillow or Facebook to write just a few sentences about your experience-and again, you can say no and it won't hurt my feelings."

You have given them out so that it isn't awkward for either of you. If they are really ambitious, you could suggest they copy and paste what they already wrote and post to all of your social media sites. Remember, this is not an essay, it's just a few words. Simply follow up with an email and the link. After hanging up with them, we write them a thank-you note to thank them for spending time on the phone with you.

Another option is that you could simply send an email (although not as personal) with the following verbiage. "Hello,_____, I was wondering if I could I get your help? A lot of people were in the same situation as you were when financing their home (first time homebuyer, credit challenges, etc.), and I find that sometime clients just need a little more reassurance when they meet a new person, in know ing that they are really and truly working with a professional. I'm wondering, and you can say no and it won't hurt my feeling, if you wouldn't mind helping me by writing a recommendation letter so that I can share your similar story with them?"

Everyone wants to help. Aren't you eager to help someone who asks you? This is the perfect time to send this email to a client. You can do the same thing with video testimonials. Perhaps consider recording your clients at the closing table.

Most will do it; however, not everyone will, so please don't get discouraged if someone doesn't. I will tell you that everybody wants to help. But one key here is you may have to do some follow up to get a recommendation or letter. Most of the time your client is going to respond letting you know they are more than willing to help. If you don't get any response, then pick up the phone and remind them about your request; that usually jogs their memory and produces results. Don't wait too long- it's better to catch them while they're still excited and everything's fresh. Even though you might have to do a little more legwork, it's worth doing.

Once you start collecting recommendation letters, pool them into different buck ets according to a potential client's situation, such as first-time homebuyers, refi nancing, credit issues, relocation, move-up buyers, reverse mortgages, second homes, investors, and so on, so that when you have a new client who fits one of those categories you can send a series of specific testimonials to reemphasize how great your business is and how you are completely capable of handling their transaction situation.

Hint: You can also capture the material from Zillow and transcribe that back into the success stories and recommendations that you send to new clients and new referral partners.

Remind them that you work by referral and appreciate them keeping you top of mind for any referrals to friends or family.

Jen's Jots

♦ Periodically write down success stories that you can then share with prospective clients and referral partners. Don't forget to enlist your team members' input.

♦ Ask for recommendations at closing or after receiving a fantastic survey.

♦ Share success stories and recommendationletters according to client situ ations, such as first-time buyers, buyers with credit issues,second homes, and so on,to demonstrate to prospective clients you have experience they can relate to.

♦ Ramp up your Zillow recommendations!

✳ Call Me...First

> **The Big Idea:** When a referral comes to you, call your referral partner first before you call the client. You may find you can help solidify the partner's relationship with the client, plus you demonstrate your willingness to help you partner's business grow.
>
> "Ask questions and identify needs before you present solutions"
>
> - Byrd Baggett

You always want to act in the interests of both your clients and your referral part ners. Well, here's a way you can do both and help further validate the relationship between you and a partner.

When a referral comes to you, what is the first thing you can do that best serves your long-term goals? Well, in my mind, the first thing you should do is check in with your referral *partner* before reaching out to the client. If you do that, you may actually then be in a position to help your referral partner win the client, as well as gain some great intel about the client so you're better prepared for the call.

Obviously, there will be times when you pick up your phone and it's a client indi cating that someone has referred them to you.

In most cases, however, you'll get a voicemail or an email from a client reaching out to you and indicating someone referred them. This is a great opportunity for you to call the referral source first to ask them if there's anything you can do to help them when you talk to the client.

One of the things that I think we take for granted is that the partner already has the client secured, That may not be the case. Sometimes they don't, sometimes they're being shopped by the client against other professionals. This presents you with a great opportunity to show you care about the partner's interests and business, You may be able to help "sell" the partner or reiterate to the client something important that the partner would like you to address,

I have found this "call the partner first"practice to be really helpful. In fact,I stum bled on this one day, and I'm now using it in the normal course of my business, What happened is that a real estate agent who made a referral happened to be in competition with four other real estate agents. When I called her, she asked me if there was anything I could say to the client to help steer the client to her. This is exactly what I did.

Of course, you can't fake your enthusiasm or the things you say. You have to know the capabilities of the partner, and you have to be familiar with how they work and how they serve their clients. That's where getting to know your referral partners more deeply can be very helpful.

If you do know your partner well, you have the opportunity to resell your refer ral partner to the client. This demonstrates in a very concrete way that you care tremendously about your referral partners and their interests.

Whether you are working with a realtor or some other referral partner, this is a great way for you to make an impact on your business.

Jen's.Jots

♦ Call your referral partner first before you call the client they referred to you.

♦ Find out from the partner if there's anything you can do or need to do to help them when you talk to the client.

♦ Helping the partner is a vivid demonstration to them that you care about their business. They will appreciate and remember what you did.

✳ The Rear-View Mirror

> **The Big Idea:** Take the time to thank each partner in the chain of referral partners that led to a client referral. This will deepen your relationships with partners and l ead to even stronger business ties.
>
> "Habits are like financial capital-forming one today is an investment that will automatically give out returns for years to come."
>
> - Shawn Achor

Do you remember the feeling you got the last time a professional acquaintance called you out of the blue to thank you for something you don't even remember doing for them? You felt really appreciated by that person, didn't you? And your positive view of that person went up a notch, maybe two, didn't it?

You probably filed away in your memory bank the goodfeeling you got from that gesture. Because of that experience, you know you're now even more likely to work with or do something for thatperson in the future.

That's the idea behind a practice I learned and implemented from Michael Maher called *The Great Retrace.* Maher is the author of *The Seven Levels of Communication:* Go *from Relationships to Referrals.*

The Great Retrace is the simple-yet very powerful-act of taking the time to thank each partner in the chain of referral partners that led to a client referral. This is something I've done for many years, and it's a great way for you to get back in touch and back to top of mind with anyone who has referred business to you in the past through the complete chain of connections thatled to the client.

Follow theLinks Backtothe Beginning

Here's how it works.

Let's say Anne, a real estate agent,just referred a prospective client. After you've had your conversation with the client, you call Anne to thank her for the refer ral. (Now this is just a bare-bones basic of our business, so I truly hope you are already taking this step.If you aren't, please, please, please make it a priority. It's the least we can do as loan officers-thank someone for referring us! When I get a referral like this,I call,I senda follow-up e-mail, andl mail a thank-you card, and/ or send a video message. This concerted follow-up is aimed at further strengthening my relationship with the partner *and* keeping me top of mind for their next prospect. Think about how you, too, can unleash a focused follow-up with referral partners.)

Now that I've closed the loop with Anne, *The Great Retrace* really gets going.

Let's say you met Anne via a referral from Bob, who happens to be a title com pany representative. You pick up the phone, call Bob, and say "Bob. I want to thank you again for referring Anne, the real estate agent to me, because she has just referred a client to me. I hope to send the client your way to get the title work completed for his transaction."

Even if there is no immediate connection for referring business to Bob, you would still call him and thank him for the referral to Anne. Now the loop is closed with Bob.

Then you would call and thank the partner who referred Bob. From there, if there is yet another connection, you'll call that person and thank them. And then every additional link in the referral chain until you get back to the beginning or don't have any more data to know who referred the initial person.

You may have only one link in your referral chain, or just two or three. The number of partners involved isn't important-what's important is that you *call every single one* so you complete the chain.

The Best Use of Your Time

These days, having been in this business as long as I have, my retrace phone call chain can go back as many as a dozen contacts. Making that many calls may seem like it takes a lot of time. You're right, sometimes it does take a fair amount of time. You know what, though, I'd rather spend the time making those calls to retrace everyone in the chain than spend that same time cold-calling or working on the minutiae of loans so that I can strengthen my relationships and perhaps jog their memory about me for yet another referral.

The retrace phone calls cement referral relationships, thus contributing to new business in the future. *The Great Retrace* is another of the many tools and tech niques you must use to bring in new leads. And as I've said over and over in these page s, lead generation is the most important activity you can do with your time.

Take the time to make those calls. The relationships you keep active and strong will pay off time and time again.

No CRM, No Retrace

Of course, making retrace phone calls back through the unbroken chain of referral partners depends on one very vital linchpin: a system for tracking the connec tions.

If you don't have, or haven't taken the time to develop a system for tracking who is sending you referrals and how you met that partner, well, you've got the great no-go. You're at a dead end. If you can't determine in a very quick, efficient way that Bob referred Anne, your chain has no links.

Your customer relationship management (CRM) system is crucial, indispensable. Without a well-maintained CRM, you don't have the system for reaching out to the right people at the right times, such as *The Great Retra ce.* You absolutely *must* have some type of CRM.

I get it that you may not have the money now to purchase a CRM system, or you may not have the time or support to manage it, but put this on your must-do list. In the meantime, put together a simple tracking system on an Excel spreadsheet so you know exactly where you're getting your referrals. Invest in your systems, and your investment will pay off many, many times over.

Jen's Jots

♦ When a partner refers a client to you, call that partner to thank them, and then call every partner in the chain of connections that led to the referral.

♦ Create a system to track how you're getting partner and prospect referrals so you know who to thank.

The Two-Way Street: Giving Business to Get Business

> **The Big Idea:** *Referring business is a two-way street. Here are key ways you can take the lead in steering clients to referral partners*
>
> *"Do you GIVE value to your customers?"*
>
> *-Anonymous*

Think of your connection to a referral partner as each of you being on the end of a two-way street. You send new business traffic in the direction of your partner, and they send new business traffic back in your direction. Sounds idyllic,right? You and your referral partners are busily sending new business back and forth to each other, and everybody's prosperous and happy.

If only! The concept makes it seem easy, but in the real world you have to be very, very proactive to pull this off. If you are proactive and you constantly send a stream of new business traffic down the street, boy are you ever going to get a lot of new business in return.

So how canyou,as a loan officer, generate clients for your referral partners'?What are some of the ways you can steer clients to real estate agents, financial plan ners, attorneys, home services providers, and on and on?

I maintain that when you send that traffic to partners you wantto be in the driver's seat. You not only want to cultivate new business for partners-so obviously they reciprocate by cultivating new business for you-but youalso want to be in con trol of howyou cultivate thatbusiness and who you send it to.

Catson a Marble Floor

Loan officers can be like cats on a marble floor, scrambling crazily for a deal,but not having any idea where they're heading. Whenever they network with a realtor, whenever they go to a broker open,whenever they go to an open house,anytime they meet a realtor, they're handing out their business card and just like that expecting business to come their way. "After all,they know <u>what</u> I do."

Then the loan officers plug the agents into their database and bug the heck out of them,but end up not doing any business with them. The problem is we always have our hands out, saying "Gimme, gimme, gimme!"

Look,there's no rule in our industry that says that I can't cultivate the client and give them *to* the realtor. And yet loan officers think they'll just *get* business from realtors, rather than *give* business. Always remember WIIFM-What's In It *From* Me?

You Are the Cross-Pollinator

One of the great things about being a loan officer is that you have the benefit (and need!) of getting the complete view of a client's financial picture. You need to talkto a client about a verywide range of financial and personal aspects when structuring a loan. Realtors don't necessarily talk to clients about all the financial aspects of borrowing. Financial planners and other partners don't necessarily talk to clients about all their goals for buying a home or about debt. As a loan officer, you can get a complete picture. If you ask the right questions and take note of what the client is telling you,you'll easily develop multiple ways to refer them to your partners.

Have a real conversation when you talk to a client about a loan. Ask them about the house; ask them about their personal or family situation as it relates to the house.

This changes the conversation from being merely about finance, money, loans, and rates to gaining trust and understanding their needs so you can also discover ways for delivering unmatched service while considering the most appropriate referral partner to refer.

You know,if you ask them about the house,they might say something like, "Oh my gosh, it's really big andyou know we can't wait.You know it's bigger than what we thought we could buy. But the kitchen's a little dated and we'll probably want to redo it and we'll most likelywant to replace the carpet too." What they've just told you includes several triggers, and when they divulge these kinds of details,you should be prepared for an opportunity to refer to one of your partners.

If I'm in that situation, I'll take note of what the client is saying so I might connect them with a kitchen cabinet re-facing contractor for now. Maybe I'll get them in touch with someone, if they have the cash, who can do a complete remodel of the kitchen. Or I can give them some ideas so they can start planning renovations for later, and a partner can slot the client as a longer-term possibility. Better yet, I could consider offering them a HELOC or renovation loan to begin with. At the very least,I've helped a partner grow their database of potential customers.

Regardless of the path, the key is to connect them with a partner who can then communicate and stay top of mind. Remember, all people have connections, friends, and family, even those with bad credit or who are not quite ready to buy.

My goal is to be introduced to them to be able to deliver value-added information and service so they will become likely to use me when they are ready and/or tell *their* connections about me too.

Every client has unique financial DNA. So as a professional mortgage lender you need to ask questions so you can pick up on the little signals and triggers. These will give you opportunities to cross-sell and refer business to a variety of referral partners.

Unfortunately, a lot of times I just don't see loan officers doing this. It is critical for your ability to refer clients to partners.

Let me shed some light on some of the possibilities you may be able to utilize:

♦ Connecting clients with an estate planner or an attorney if they don't have a will. That partner can eventually upsell them to creating a trust.

♦ Connecting them with a financial advisor if the clients have multiple 401k accounts from previous jobs. The financial advisor can work with them to consolidate and rebalance their accounts.

♦ With a new home purchase, their finances may warrant connecting them with a CPA for tax advice. This is especially the case if they plan to hold onto their existing home as a rental. Remember that tax benefits are dif ferent for investors.

♦ Connecting clients to a variety of partners such as home services for reno vations or updates, personal services in their new neighbo rhood, or finan cial services to continue to develop their estate planning.

Take a moment to think about the DNA of your past five or six clients financial situations. I bet you could come up with a potential 15 or 20 referrals you could have made-and can make right now.

Put Yourself in the Driver's Seat

There are several ways to put yourself in the driver's seat so that you can steer business to referral partners.

One very key way that works for me is to conduct seminars on a range of topics: from first-time buyers, sellers, credit repair, move up buyers and sellers, investors, all the way to wealth building in real estate. These seminars enable me to cultivate a relationship with consumers directly, which then enables me to guide potential clients to real estate agents and other referral partners. This puts me in control of the referral instead of the partner being in control.

Seller seminars have become very important in recent years because sellers who haven't sold a house since before the Great Recession often don't have a realistic outlook of what it takes to sell a house these days. You know, years ago, before the credit crunch, you didn't have to do anything to sell your house. You could put your house on the market at midnight and quite literally at 12:01 a.m. you would have multiple offers with escalation clauses. You didn't have to do anything to get your home ready to sell either. Numerous sellers still think the same way today.

Most sellers haven't been back in the market for years. They were upside down or they stayed in their house longer because they refinanced a time or two, or for whatever reason, just didn't move. Now with all the compliance and regulations, they're entering a market that can be like visiting a foreign country where nobody speaks their language.

On top of that, today's sellers have to come to terms with selling to the new era of homebuyer. And what's the issue with selling these days, you may ask? Well, buyers want everything *perfect*. It must have a perfect kitchen and have high-end appliances, and then there are the upgrades that go without saying. These expec tations are something that some sellers may simply not be prepared for.

This new market situation creates opportunities to hold a seminar series for just sellers. For example, once a month for a number of months on a Saturday morn ing, I and a real estate partner conduct a seminar that covers varying issues on how to sell a home in today's real estate world. Each month I bring in a presenter to address a different aspect of home selling. One month it might be a landscaper to talk about curb appeal, or a home stager to talk to them about why staging is now such an important part of selling, or a home inspector to talk to them about how today's buyers will inspect absolutely everything in a house. During the course of the series, the agent gets new listings and sales, I get new sales and refinances; and I also have new clients to refer to other partners as well.

My message is that you have to look for opportunities to cultivate new business on your own, or in tandem with a real estate agent partner.

Another powerful way that I cultivate business for myself as well as for real estate agents is to hold lunch-and-learns at businesses where a client works. Every bor rower works some place,- obviously they have to have income to get a loan- and they usually have coworkers who may also be in the market to buy a home.

So if you do 100 loans a year, that means you have a potential connection to 100 different organizations that employ people who make enough money to buy a house. That's 100 organizations that you can reach out to in order to pitch a quar terly or monthly lunch-and-learn. You can get in touch with the HR dep artment, or even the president if it's a smaller company, to propose a lunch-and-lean series for their employees. (You can let them know that an employee recently got a loan through you, and you would love the opportunity to teach other employees about what they need to know when buying a home. Of course, you can' t divulge the name of the employee due to privacy protections.)

For the lunch-and-learns that I conduct, I spearhead the program and bring in a variety of speakers,from real estate agents, to financial planners, to life insurance agents and CPAs, to provide them with access to potential new clients. I typi cally ask the speaker/partner to provide lunch as well. We give presentations on financing a home, such as "Everything you thought you knew about mortgages but don't." As the organizer, I have now become the "giver." I'm giving my partners access to potential new clients and at the same time providing them the opportu nityfor increased exposure.

As I said, some organizations will agree to a monthly series, some want to do it quarterly, some wantto do it semi-annually.I don't really care,the key thing is that every week, I'm providing a lunch-and-learn by myself or with a partner some where. The lunch-and-learns are cultivating a direct relationship with consumers,
allowing me the chance to guide them directly to the partners of my choosing, and I'm now in control of the referral.

This same philosophy works with first-time buyer's seminars, first-time seller's seminars, basically any kind of educational seminar that puts you in the driver's seat.

Jen's Jots

♦ As a loan officer, you can be a cross-pollinator, matching a client's needs to a wide variety of referral partners if you take the time to get to know their needs.

♦ Ask questions. Have conversations with your clients so you can identify signals and triggers that open up referral possibilities.

♦ Sponsor events, such as seminars and lunch-and-learns, to cultivate a direct relationship with clients to generate your own business and be able to guide clients to referral partners.

♦ Always follow-up immediately with a new connection to continue the con versation.

✳ Tag Along

> **The Big Idea:** Involve a partner in networking events that you have access to so you can both benefit from potential new connections, and ask them to do the same for you
>
> "1+ 1=11(Power in Numbers)"
>
> -Lou Holts

When we think about networking, as loan officers we invariably think about going by ourselves to whatever event we've targeted. We do a lot of networking through BNIs, Chambers, women's groups, and other kinds of groups, but we always tend to go by ourselves, And that's fine, because we have to continue making new connections to keep our practice strong and ever growing,

Will going alone to a networking event give you the most benefit? Maybe not. What if you paired up with a partner, particularly a real estate agent, to attend a networking event where that partner might make new connections that could then lead back to more business for you?

This is something I'm doing more of, and I recommend it for you also,

It came about because of a year-end meeting I had with one of my top real estate partners. These year-end meetings are something I do to determine if a partner's goals are continuing or changing and to make sure I can still be an important part of their plans.

This partner mentioned that one thing she was trying to move toward is working more with affluent buyers and sellers, and during the year she hadn't made the progress that she had hoped to make. I told her I also wanted to do more business in that market and I too hadn't had a chance to work on ways to increase the number of affluent buyers I work with,

This conversation got us to thinking about ways we could work on this together, We realized that co-networking could be a great solution,

If you want to get the most benefit from asking a real estate agent to tag along with you to networking events, you need to know what their interests are and what kind of clients they will attract and are trying to attract. You need to know what makes their ears perk up. You need to know a lot about them.

You may be friends with a real estate agent online on Facebook or LinkedIn, but you need to dig deeper with them and learn more about them, about what they like to do and about the kinds of activities they're involved in. Knowing what they like to do and what they participate in gives you a better perspective of their target market.

Let's say you have a connection with a real estate agent who mentions how much she likes boating and she shows you pictures of her and her family out on a boat. You should ask about networking together at events at which there are people interested in boating so that you can meet some of the people she's networking with. You may be involved in a group that includes a certain type of client the real estate agent is interested in meeting. You then can take the agent to that group's events where she can potentially meet these clients. Your joint efforts will lead to more business for both of you, both directly and through referrals.

So find out what your partners, especially your real estate partners, absolutely love to do, and then go do it with them. Invite them to networking events that include the types of clients they are focusing on. Bring someone to an event who you think you could really help, because by helping their business they will help yours.

Jen's Jots

♦ Identify a partner's interests and the types of clients they are trying to attract.

♦ Co-network with the partner at events you have access to and which attract the type of client the partner is seeking.

♦ Co-network with the partner at events they have access to and which attract the type of client you are seeking.

✳ Finder Tasks/Roles/Activities

The Big Idea: *Sample list of Finder Activities to get you started "The Compounding effect to Relational Selling is the 8th Wonder of the World"*

-Albert Einstein

♦ Milestone updates to clients and partners.

♦ Interview/Meet with potential referral partners.

♦ Attend open houses/broker opens.

♦ Make outbound calls to top partners.

♦ Sales visits with past clients and referral partners.

♦ Following up on leads for nurturing and conversion.

♦ Make outbound lead generating calls.

♦ Business planning and vision.

♦ Presentations.

♦ Attend events and networking.

♦ Problem solving as needed.

♦ Prepare and record videos for clients and partners.

♦ Weekly planning review with team.

♦ Talent scout.

♦ Initial loan structure and consultation.

♦ Restructure of loan terms and communicate with clients when necessary.

♦ Daily huddle withteam members.

♦ Hold events and client appreciation parties.

♦ Socializing al networking events.

♦ Hosting client and referral partner appreciation events.

♦ Marketing to your database for more referrals.

- Attend closings/settlements.
- Teach classes (continuing education as well).
- Conducting a discovery meetings with clients.
- Loan analysis.
- Strategy sessions with clients.

SECTION 5.
MINDER

✳ The Maestro

> **The Big Idea:**You can't do it all by yourself. Consider how you can leverage a team to accomplish your goals
>
> "Discipline is the foundation upon which all success is built Lack of discipline inevitably leads to failure."
>
> -JimRohn

The Minder role is so important in allowing you to keep focused on Finder activi ties rather than being pulled back into the office to complete tasks that don't generate business, but are equally as important, in order to maintain the seNice levels you want to provide. You can also reference this role as the Relationship Manager because this person keeps everyone happy. you,the client,realtor, and other team members throughout the loan process.

What do you do when you hit a brickwall in your career or your practice, you find yourself at a breaking point, and you just can't continue putting in long hours and keep up the pace any longer?

Well, you will want to start *leveraging* resources in whatever manner you define. That may mean hiring an assistant if you are currently on your own, or it may mean leveraging more productivity out of your team by better identifying all the right roles for each team member, or leveraging more referrals out of your referral partners by asking better questions.

WhenEnough isEnough

Looking back, I can recall the biggest brick wall that I hit and what helped me through, at least on the origination side of things, to be a powerhouse and only do what was in my genius zone.

I was closing 18 loans a month. I couldn't get past 18. Even though I had enough loans in my pipeline to do so, physically I couldn't get past 18. At the time,I was a lender located in a real estate office and working until 11:00 at night. No matter what I did, I could never close 19 loans in a month. I had hit a glass ceiling for months on end!

My turning point was that I realized and concealed the fact that I absolutely needed to hire someone to help me. Prior to this point, I couldn't bring myself to do it. After all, my clients and referral partners wanted ME, not some other person. I had to let my ego go or I was going to drop dead. This is the thought many of us have until we reach a breaking point when enough is enough. You feel like you built it, and therefore, everybody wants you, but really what they want is the experience they get by working with you.

I have news for you. As you get more and more business in your pipeline, you begin to drop balls. In fact, someone said to me not too long ago that there's a dif ference between juggling balls and juggling glass balls. I thought that was really important to understand, because when you're juggling a lot of balls for a while, eventually they become glass balls. If you drop something and it breaks, it could be detrimental to your business. So as a result, you work longer and harder hours to make sure that you're keeping all those glass balls in the air.

But honestly, what's happening is you're hurting yourself physically, you're hurting yourself emotionally, and the odds are you're most likely hurting your relationship with your family. I strongly urge you to look at the quality of your business, not the quantity, but the quality of the business that you're doing right now. Because you're probably not running at 100 percent capacity. Most likely you're running at, let's say, 40 or 60 percent capacity. And yet I hear from everyone, "I don't want to hire anyone because I can just do it better myself. I can't find someone who is a mini-me."

Well, you don't want a mini-you. A mini-you is someone who's performing at 40 to 60 percent. What you want is to hire someone who can do it better than you! And if you can find someone who can perform at 100 percent, fantastic! Even someone who can perform the task at 80 percent capacity is better than you because you may only be working and functioning at 40 or 60 percent capacity.

Now, if you are functioning at 100 percent capacity, with all these glass balls in the air, working until 11:00 at night, then you have to ask yourself is it worth it? No free time, loss of family time, etc. All the money you are making, you're not enjoying one bit! When are you going to take time off? I'm coaching someone now who just doesn't want to take vacation because if she does, she thinks everything's going to fall through the cracks. She doesn't trust her team. She either doesn't have the right people on her team, doesn't trust herself, takes on too much of the process herself, or hasn't effectively led, trained, or developed her team. As a result, she won't take time off. She can't enjoy the money she's making.

Back to my turning point. I was working until 11:00 at night and then driving 54 miles home from my office. Welcome to "Hotel Home!" And then I'd need to get up early after no sleeping through the night, since I was worrying about every thing .

I was working on everybody else's time, everybody else's schedule, doing lots of loans, and everyone loved the service I was providing, but I was killing myself to do it. I finally said enough is enough! What I was doing to myself was not worth the money. I was making $70,000-$80,000 per month, but who cared? It wasn't worth my health or my emotions. And my entire identity was as a mortgage lender-nothing else but a mortgage lender, 24/7, even while I was sleeping, or at least trying to sleep.

And that was my tipping point. I said, you know what, I need hire somebody, I have to. And this was eye-opening. In the weeks after I made that hire, I didn't get to just 19 loans a month, which had been my goal. Instead, I jumped to 25 and 26 loans a month (yet another operations issue to resolve). And I saw right away the first month that the position was paying for itself.

Remember that whatever it is that you do that keeps people coming back can be duplicated with a great team and systems. Of course, you do have to worry about hiring the right person, about identifying and understanding your goals, and fitting this person into your perfect loan process.

Whatever your situation, your solution-your leverage point-might be the same as what I discovered mine was. I realized that/ *hadto get outof myownwayin order to be successful.* It was simply costing me money, and my lifestyle, not to hire a Minder.

The bottom line is, we are sales people. We should not be in operations, and by getting involved too much in the loan transaction process, we're in operations. If you choose to be involved in operations, your income will be capped. Instead, choose to leverage additional help so you can be in sales, and then the sky's the limit!

Jen's Jots

♦ Apply the resources available to you to maximum your success-don't try to go it alone.

♦ Your effectiveness will be in direct proportion to the resources you can leverage to advance your practice.

✳ The Maestro

> **The Big Idea:** With your perfect loan process in place, you can manage client communications and expectations to deliver a Wow customer experience.
>
> *"Excellence is not optional."*
>
> *-Anonymous*

Exceed Expectations

About 25 years ago,I was attending a mortgage event to learn about mortgage backed securities, taught by Barry Habib. If you've been in the business long enough,I'm sureyou remember his events. While sitting there with over 100 other loan officers (99% men at that time), I noticed that each of their pagers were going off left and right-yes, pagers. I thought how important and busy they must have been because so many were running in and out of the seminar to handle business. So, thinking that I should act the partin advance of having the success, the next time I attended an event, I asked my husband, Brian, to page me five times during the course of the 3-hour session. I was in! I looked busy, needed, and important. Check me out-I'm having to get up and leave the meeting too! Only thing was that after I stood in line to use the payphone like all the others, my conversations were with Brian about the kids' activities and what we were having for dinner, I didn't have the business at the time, but boy did I sure wish I looked like I did.

Fast forward several years andI found myself managing many of the loan officers who attended those events with me. What did I discover? I discovered that they not only didn't have as much business as I thought, but in fact had the same amount of business as I did at the time-they simply didn't have control of their process! What a life lesson. I learned that it isn't always what it seems,

I immediately began developing a process that would allow me to attend events without the chaos that came with constant phone calls and pages. This was the beginning of me building the systems and processes for team development that I use today.

An important aspect of client satisfaction is to create strong advocates by exceeding expectations. Since expectations can vary widely from one client to the next,take extra time to have a conversation with them, While you will have an iron-clad system being executed, you still must educate them as to what to expect during the loan process. And, of course,exceptionally satisfied customers send more referrals.

You need to have a conversation to tellyour clients how things are going to go. If you have that conversation withthem at the beginning, they won't be wondering what the next step is or whether they should call you for an update. Take a few minutes up front to go through the entire process,because during the processing of the loanyou won't have to answer the same questions repeatedly. Once again, another time saver.

Perception is everything. In a 2016 suNey of 362 businesses conducted by Bain & Company research firm, 80% of the companies surveyed state they deliver a "'superior'" customer experience, while only 8% of their clients agreed. 8%! Seriously, what we think doesn't matter, but what clients think matters tremen dously.

Let's look at those two intertwined elements: having a process in place that keeps you on top of every detail of the loan process, and defining the expectations with the client as to what willhappen, when, and why during the process.

Build It andThey WillCome

Of course,to be able to explain your process, you first need a process in pl ace! I know this sounds obvious to many of you. But I also know there are many mort gage loan people who don't have a predefined, step-by-step, repeatable *system* in place for transaction management and customer service during the transac tion. While on this topic, as I mentioned earlier, think strongly about developing systems for all aspects of your practice (for example, leads, active and passive prospects, credit repair, partners,client retention, etc.)

Remember, if you don't have a system in place,you have leaks. And if you have leaks,you run the risk of having dissatisfied clients.

If your system isn't air-tight, or if, heaven forbid,you haven't defined a system, this is the first irreplaceable step in exceeding customer expectations. Define and follow a system so thatyou can anticipate any customer question or need, so you and your team can always stay a step ahead of anything that a customer thinks about.

Steve Dorfman, my companies' Chief eXperience Officer, reminds us that custom ers don't go to customer school. They don't always know what to expect, so it's our job to help them understand. For example,I created a checklist for my borrow ers so that at every step theyknow exactly where they are in the process. There are 46 points of information on the checklist, and we send them an email showing the checklist with the completed items marked off. Every time they receive an email from us, it shows them how far along they are in the process. It simply mir rors the information we have provided to them.

Whatever information or way you provide the information during your process, give clients a checklist so they can follow along and see where they are in the process. You can also use the checklist to help trigger action that is needed on their part. For example, after receipt of an appraisal, the clients need to finalize their homeowner's insurance.

Proactive communication teaches you to anticipate what a client might ask right before they ask it. A great system should alert you to upcoming milestones in the process so you can touch base with a client before they contact you for an update. This demonstrates to them that you're in charge and in control of the process.

I've always been an advocate for milestone updates rather than the traditional weekly updates most loan officers and teams subscribe too. If anything, do both.

Setting Expectations with Clients

The second part of this equation is that you should explain to the client exactly what to expect and when. It is your job to educate them on how the process will play out, how you will manage it through your systems, and how you will consis tently communicate with them at each milestone while also providing them with "next steps."

Your goal, really, is to never get a phone call from a client asking you what the status of their loan is and what's happening next. You should possess the desire for inbound calls to be dedicated only to new referrals. That's right, your goal is to NEVER get a phone call asking you what's next.

There are a couple of reasons for this. First, if you get a phone call like that, you've failed to exceed client service expectations. If they have to ask, you're not on top of the situation. Your system should be helping you manage expectations so that you're always reaching out one step ahead of the client.

The second reason you never want clients calling to ask what's next is that these incoming calls are defensive calls. They are setbacks-like a football sack. You have to take extra time in your day to respond to them, and frankly if you disen gage from the process, you may need to take valuable time to research a ques tion or make phone calls. This is time you could be using to prospect for new business! So now you'd have two strikes against you: the client has to contact you *and* you're using up valuable time that could be redirected to bringing in more business.

Lastly, for quality communication, ask your client how they want to be communi cated with, and when. Do they want texts, do they want phone calls, do they want emails? Do they want you to talk to the husband and not the wife or vice versa, or alw ays both? Are there other people who are going to be involved in the decision making and the process? Find these things out at the beginning when you're explaining to them how everything is going to work.

Setting Expectations Helps Your Partners

In addition to setting expectations with your clients and staying ahead of their questions, you can provide tremendous value to your referral partners as well. One, a strong iron-clad system differentiates you from your competition, and two, a great process should keep your referral partner updated so they can focus on their practice and not yours. Sharing with your partners on how you're going to communicate with their clients during the loan process also pays great dividends.

Collaborate with your partner about the frequency in which you'll communicate with them while a property is under contract. Even if nothing is happening, you may agree that you'll call once a week to keep them abreast of the situation. It lets them know you're handling the process and they don't have to worry about it.

It'sSimply About Communication

With a comprehensive system in place, the linchpin to customer satisfaction is simply communication. In fact, with a system behind you, I'll bet you could reach nearly 100 percent in client satisfaction. I read a report by CoreLogic that reported that when mortgage lenders reach out and communicate with customers during the loan process, client satisfaction reaches the 90 percent level. When lenders don't communicate, the satisfaction level drops to 40 percent! That is a huge spread!

Again, your communication should be anticipatory when directing your clients. Recognize pending speed bumps. Be aware of the level of frustration a client may be experiencing. Set up triggers to have conversations-don't rely solely on automation. Let your gut guide you. If you're *not* ahead of the client's anticipated needs, you'll get a gut feeling, a sense that you're not communicating to the level that you need to be. You might get the sense that there's something that's starting to drift away from you. (Hopefully, you never, ever experience this feeling, but if you do, take steps to correct it immediately!)

In those cases, pick up the phone and take action. Our natural tendency is to think the issue will fix itself. But the situation can escalate. It's better to have these com munication points incorporated into your process and explained right from the beginning. That's why I have such an extensive communication process.

Jen's Jots

♦ Client satisfaction begins with having a well-thought-out system to manage the transaction processes and communication with clients.

♦ Create a system that enables you to anticipate any question or client need so you can remain in control.

♦ People don't go to customer school;help them every step of the way.

✳ Build an Effective Team

> **The Big Idea:** *Bring out the best in your team through careful selection to maximize their roles and then effective delegation.*
>
> *'You are more brilliant when you admitit and ask for help!"*
>
> *- Jen Du Plessis*

Previously, I talked about how your wider success may depend on how you free yourself of daily Minding and Grinding activities so that you can concentrate on lead generating activities. Climbing the ladder of success means that there will be a need to hire people to supportyou.

If you recall,I talked about how you can'tcovet and hold onto every task, because it prevents you from making your business scalable. At some point, you have to give up tasks that got you where you are today and pass them to someone else to handle.

Here's the question I asked you: What do you need to let go of so you canclimb the ladder of success? The sooner you decide, the faster you're going to get there.

As you climb higher and your practice grows, your team will have to grow. That means you'll need to regularly focus on team building because eventually your needs will change.

A Holistic View of Team Building

Before we talk about the roles of your team members, let's frame whatteam build ing means. Team building is not just about hiring some people. It encompasses the growth, development, and management of people and their work culture. Team building is about creating an environment, an ecosystem if you will, that takes into account everybody and everything within that environment.

The principal elements of team building are:

♦ Recruiting, selecting, and hiring the right people.
♦ Managing team performance and training.

- ◆ Creating and managing a team culture.
- ◆ Team communication.

Recruiting, selecting, and hiring the right people starts with determining your opti mum role and determining the optimum roles of the people you bring on to assist you.

Leadership

Ideally, if you are the *Finder* in your practice, you spend your time, energy, and activities to grow the revenue for your practice. Everything else should be del egated to your team members.

The *Minder* is the person who makes sure that the loan process runs smoothly by providing exemplary customer service and communication; collects and reviews financial documents received from the borrower, and reviews the documents. The *Minder* is the person who is doing all those activities because you can't serve your clients properly by spreading yourself too thin. Your *Minder* needs to be the per son who is scheduling appointments, who is watching and looking at your emails, and is responding quickly to requests by borrowers while you are building your business and bringing in more loans.

The *Minder* is also the conductor of your orchestra, ensuring all "musicians" (team members) are working at their best and are fully informed about their roles. This includes safeguarding that pertinent deadlines are met and the loan is always moving forward.

Then there's the *Grinder,* your database manager and/or marketing director. They prepare mailers, database entry, packages for classes and seminars, posting on social media, etc.

All the roles on your team must be defined, and you should match a person's capabilities and personality with the defined duties. If you're just starting out to assemble a team, one way to do this is to keep a list of activities. Start writing down all the various tasks you do. This goes WAY back in my tenure when we used to write down every 15 minutes what we were doing. I'm not saying to do that, I'm just saying that whenever you do something, write it down, whether it's printing, reviewing a paystub, meeting a real estate agent one-to-one, or attend ing a networking event. Whatever the activity or task, take note so you can later categorize each into either a Finder, Minder, or Grinder role. Quickly, you'll find that you've already developed job descriptions for each.

Delegate Effectively for Max Results

You have to match people and roles. It won't help you advance your practice if an assistant doesn't thrive in their roles and duties. You also must set them up for success by training them for the job and then effectively delegating the work to them. You have to trust the team you put in place so that you don't hover and you don't try to control every move they make. Remember, they are there to take work and activities off your shoulders so you can focus on one thing: building your practice.

You know, some of us need lessons on how to delegate. It may not be something that comes easy to you, or because you have difficulty letting go. Look at delega tion as an opportunity to free up more of your valuable time. When you delegate, look for tasks that are preventing you from accomplishing your principal role. First, pick these things to delegate. Here are a few statements to assist you in recogniz ing when delegating is needed:

♦ What you don't know how to do.

♦ What you're not good at.

♦ What doesn't directly generate money for you.

♦ What's falling through the cracks.

♦ What you don't have time for.

It also helps to identify the things you don't like to do, the things you like to do, and the things only you can do. This exercise will help you sort out what activities must be put in your team's hands and what you keep in your hands.

There are a couple of other important points about delegating to keep in mind.

Don't be a bottleneck in your business! Get out of your team's way. If they know their role and what it is they're supposed to do, let them do it. Don't hover and don't try to insert yourself where you shouldn't be.

By the same token, don't expect your team members to do what you want them to do if you haven't set up a system for them and you haven't trained them. Don't just fling activities and assignments at them if you have n't first sat down with them, explained the activity's place in your process and practice, and talked about the results you expect.

First, you must establish the framew ork and then let them work within the system and expectations you've developed. Otherwise, you'll just end up throwing some thing at them to do, watching them as they flail, and then end up doing it yoursel.f This isn't maximizing your team.

One effective way to train your team members is to document everything you do and how to do it. Within the framework of your system, establish procedur es and the results that must be achieved with these procedures. A handy way to explain something once and then not have to go backto it again is to make a recording of it. For example, use screen capture software such as Camtasia to record yourself doing an activity and talking through the activity's steps. You only have to do this one time as you record it, and then it's always available for any team member to review or for new team members to watch and learnfrom.

Jen's Jots

♦ When building a team,first define roles and then match a person's capa bilities and personality with their id eal role.

♦ Delegate responsibilities and then step out of the way so your team can do their job. Empower them.

♦ When delegating, look specifically at actions that arepreventing you from accomplishing your principal role on the team.

✳ Ensure a Clearly Defined Handoff

> **The Big Idea:** Make a clean hand-off of a loan to your Minder. Don't constantly hover as the loan moves through its processing you need to be finding new loans
>
> "Experience is simply the name we give to our mistakes"
>
> - Oscar Wilde

Something that many loan officers struggle with is conducting a solid and clear hand-off of the client to their mortgage planner/assistant. I'm frequently asked, "How do you perform the hand-off of the client to my team?"

It's an important question. As the *Finder* in your practice, after you've worked with a client to structure the loan and the loan terms, and gain their commitment to work with you, it is imperative that you hand off the loan and the client to your assistant or team for the next steps so you can return your attention to finding more new business. In other words, you need to make a smooth hand-off to the *Minder* in your practice.

Get the Loan in Place

Whether you have just one assistant or a team, you must have a smooth process to accomplish this transfer, and, of course, confidence in your assistant or team.

Let me tell you briefly what works for me. You don't have to do it this way, but this is how it works for me.

When I receive a referral from a referral partner, say a real estate agent or a financial planner, I work with the client exclusively. My goal is to lead the loan development as the Certified Mortgage Planner; there's no one else who can do that better on my team since not everyone on my team is a Certified Mortgage Planner.

I work with the client to structure the loan and the loan terms, and once they have chosen the best loan product and terms to meet their needs and goals, I then have a quick conversation with the client sharing the important of my position, as well as upselling my team members because of their expertise in a specific area. In fact,if I were to get involved with answering routine questions, I would most likely make a mess of the entire process.

Once the client finds a home, makes an offer, and goes under contract, I will quickly reach out to the client to make sure that the terms have not changed, discuss any changes that would affect them, and provide next steps. From that point on I refer the loan over to my *Minder*. He takes it from there. He prepares all the disclosures, sends them to the client for signature, and manages their timely return. In the odd case that I'm meeting the client to sign disclosures, my *Minder* will provide them.

From receipt of the contract, or decision to refinance, I'm not involved in the loan until maybe we lock in the rate. I'm usually involved in that either in the very beginning or as we progress through, depending on what's happening with the market.

A Clean Hand-off Wins

You can visualize this process as a relay race. In track, the baton hand-off is where relay races are won or lost. The transfer has to be clean and consistent every time. Just like in your practice!

You run the first leg of the race, then hand off the baton to your *Minder*. But you need to remember to let go. No one likes a "helicopter loan officer." I think this transition is where problems crop up. You hand the baton to your assistant and they may have to drag you along with them because you're not willing to let go. Or the hand-off is a little sloppy because you don' t give clear guidance, and the baton drops and the whole race is a mess. Or you hand off the baton but then run alongside as a helicopter loan officer, making sure that everything goes smoothly. Perhaps as bad, you hand the baton to your assistant and then walk out of the stadium instead of watching what happens in the next part of the race in an effort to support your team.

You certainly can hand off the baton and watch it go around the rest of the track, progressing from your *Minder* to your processor to underwriting. If anything gets dropped, or things are moving too slowly, you can certainly jump in at that point to guide your team and bring them back from their drifting. But your job is to start the race, hand it off cleanly, go back to the beginning, and start the process again. That is the essence of lead generation and that's really what the *Finder's* role is. Make a clean hand-off, get yourself out of the paperwork, and stop hovering. Get back to finding new business.

Jen's Jots

♦ After you work with a client to get a loan's structure and terms into place, make a clean hand-off of the client and loan to your assistant or team.

♦ If you trust the system you have in place, stop hovering over the loan processing and get back to finding new business.

♦ If you don't trust your system, improve your system!

✳ Don't Go Dark

> **The Big Idea:** Make sure you have a system in place to communicate regularly with a client as their loan is working its way through the process.
>
> "The customer's perception IS reality."
>
> -Anonymous

The period between a client's decision to work with you and closing can be a sensitive, stressful, and overwhelming time for a client.

This is precisely when communication with the parties involved, external and internal, is so crucial. Please don't go dark during this time! It's so easy to move on to the next loan, but your work isn't done.

Everyone wants to stay updated, even if there is no news. If you go dark because you think you don't have anything to tell them, that's not good. It's going to have a negative effect on the client's experience, a client you probably worked very hard to get.

Do you remember those talent shows where the noise level of clapping by the audience sent the needle, the arrow, all the way to one side? The less you communicate with everyone during this nervous and trying time, the more their love o-meter will start pointing the wrong way.

When you're communicating and keeping everyone informed at each milestone in the process, the needle on their love-o-meter will continue to tilt in the right direction, registering high satisfaction. When your communication is lagging, the love-o-meter needle is sagging. It might sink all the way back to zero, at which point you have to start building trust all over again.

I also call this rising and waning faith in you the trust account. Any communication with a client or referral partner either deposits or withdrawals from the trust account, based on the experience the client just had with you. Every communication that you or your team have with that client throughout the whole process-every communication, the tone of the email, responsiveness, availability, whether you're in a good mood or a bad mood, the digital manner in which you communicate with your client-either makes deposits or makes withdrawals from that trust account.

Slow down enough to recognize when your client may be becoming frustrated. Maybe they received the disclosures and no one on your team called them to review. Instead, they may ultimately have to painstakingly work through the end less pages on their own. Perhaps no one has called them for some time and they don't know where they are in the process. That love-o-meter needle is sputtering and sagging as you go dark. And that is not good.

And if something is going wrong in the process or something is held up, that's really the time to keep them up-to-date. If you don't have answers for the client because you have to check with anunderwriter or a manager, you really need to keep them posted every step of the way. Unless, of course,you want the trust account to be completely drained! They simply don't want to be kept in the dark.
If you don't have an answer, callthem and tell them that. If you know when you'll have an answer, call them and tellthem when it will be.

And don't hide behind keyboard confidence! Just one simple phone call is all it takes sometimes, even if there's nothing to say and everything is going great.

When things are running smoothly, that might be the time to do something original and unexpected, such as sending a video message via email. You can deliver a positive message "in person," andthatwill gomiles and miles toward them being very happy with you,your team, and your company and service.

Constantly anticipating their questions and communicating in a systematized way (a drip campaign) throughout the entire process speaks volumes about your ser vice, care, and character.

Note: Make sure your clients and partners don't forget that you are always seek ing referrals. Every time you have the opportunity to call them-whether it's to talk about disclosures, or submittal, or conditional approval, or appraisal, or receiving the clear to close-it is an opportunity to remind them that you appreciate refer rals and want referrals. If you're not communicating in a system-driven way,you're foregoing a lot of opportunities for referrals. Not to negate the fact that when you first meet them,that's the best time to set the tone about referrals.

Confirm that your team or your processor-everybody-follows your system for touching base with the client at the times predetermined in your system. You and your team are either always depositing or withdrawing from the trust account, so for God's sake be consistent.

All of this advice also goes for communicating with your referral partners during the loan process. You are depositing or withdrawing everytime you communicate or don't communicate with them. As you're going through the loan process, keep in mind that you want to take similar actions so they don't feel in the dark about their client-their referral.

Jen's Jots

♦ An important component of your loan process is a predefined system for communicating with a client to keep them informed and happy.

♦ Communicate even when nothing is going on and there are no develop ments to report. Anticipate a client's apprehension when they don't hear from you.

✳ Opportunity Knocking

> **The Big Idea:** *Build automatic steps into your Minding process that will then help you build your business.*
>
> *"Practicing on clients is VERY expensive."*
>
> *-Anonymous*

There are countless ways to constantly grow your practice. Some of them are simple, easy-to-do steps that should be automatic in your process for either a *Finder* or *Minder* to complete.

For example, when you receive a contract from a listing agent who you haven't worked with in the past, create an automated process to reach out to them. I hear loan officers say that when a contract comes in they call occasionally and intro duce themselves to the listing agent, but they're not doing it consistently.

This is a task that must be done 100 percent of the time. It's a great way for you to filter out and strategically decide if a new listing agent, whom you've never heard of, will be someone thatyou're going to allow as one of your partners. If they bring too much drama to you or your team,they shouldn't be part of your sphere.

As soon as the contract comes in, go ahead and review it before calling the listing agent to make sure you know all the pertinent dates and deadlines for financing contingency and appraisal contingency. Then give them a quick call and let them know something along the lines of this, "Hi,*listing agent,* this is Jen Du Plessis. I just wanted to let you know that I've had a chance to review the contract in its entirety. I don't have any questions about the content thus far, but I wanted you to know thatI've made note of all the pertinent dates and contingency deadlines and my team and I will be working toward those dates to ensure that we have a smooth closing."

This is a great way to just introduce yourself to the listing agent and see if there are any questions or comments from them. You may find that they have removed the lockbox, revealing an opportunity for you to communicate with the appraisal management company to notify them that the lockbox was removed so they will need to contact the listing agent to gain access to the property.

Another reason to call the listing agent is to discuss the appraisal process. Remind them that all appraisals are ordered through an Appraisal Management Company and that you are not allowed to have communication with the appraiser (you don't even know who will be assigned to inspect the property or who will be the inspector), to have comparables available for the appraisal that support the listing agent's decision to place the home on the market at the price they did,and finally discussing the timing of receipt of the appraisal and your companies' process for reviewing and approving.

As soon as you're done with the phone call, write a quick thank-you note to the agent telling them you're ready and capable to provide a smooth closing.

Now, the second thing is that sometime during the process, and you can decide when this is best for you, send an email to the listing agent to say that you'd like the opportunity to meet with them sometime during the loan process. Why wait until after closing? They don't think they need you any further. You can tell them you'd like to give them an understanding of how your business works. You'd like to see if there's an opportunity for you to share more about how you can provide value and increase their business.

This is not an opportunity to do an info dump about you and your practice and all the programs that you offer. Instead, focus on sharing a testimonial from another real estate agent or a success story about a client,providing them with ideas for how you can help their business grow, expose their brand, or how you create smooth transactions with your perfect loan process, allowing them to focus on their role instead of interfering with your duties during the process.

This is a simple way for you to make animpact on your mortgage practice. Callthe listing agent as soon as you have had a chance to review the contract, followed by a thank you note, send them an email, at a later point during the process, ask ing for a short meeting with them to see if there's some way that youcan impact and create value for their business.

Jen's Jots

♦ When a contract is received and the listing agent is new to you, have a system for introducing yourself and your practice,to begin the process of determining if you have mutual grounds for a business relationship.

♦ Discuss the appraisal process so expectations are clear.

♦ Follow this up right away with a thank-you card.

♦ Follow up during the loan process with an email requesting a one-to-one meeting to begin exploring a future business relationship.

✳ Minder Tasks/Roles/Activities

> **The Big Idea:** Sample listof Minder activities to get you started.
>
> *"Knowledge without application is useless"*
>
> *-Anonymous*

- ◆ You are the Maestro for communication.
- ◆ Manage updates to all parties.
- ◆ Obtain initial financial documents.
- ◆ Loan placement analyst.
- ◆ Review contract.
- ◆ Manage and monitor deadlines.
- ◆ Run LP/DU and all revisions.
- ◆ Prepare pre-approval letter.
- ◆ Prepare file for initial disclosures.
- ◆ Manage disclosure signing.
- ◆ Manage digital file folders.
- ◆ Request for rush,exceptions, waiver of fees.
- ◆ Initial problem solving with processor.
- ◆ Prepare and manage change of circumstances.
- ◆ Communicate & approval final CD with processor.
- ◆ Run credit.
- ◆ Complete application details with client.
- ◆ Daily huddle.
- ◆ Additional tasks if licensed:
- ◆ Initial conversation with leads for Finder.
- ◆ Write thank-you notes.
- ◆ Lead management.
- ◆ Prepare Mortgage Coach Edge.

SECTION 6.
GRINDER

✳ The Team Supporter

> **The Big Idea:** Without a Grinder, you can expect to spend countless hours working in your business and not on your business, or letting too many actionable items slip through the cracks.
>
> "The name of the Magic Pill for success is called 'Hard Work:'"
>
> -Anonymous

Wow! I can't possibly imagine my practice running without an effective *Grinder*. These days, there is so much emphasis on the importance of our database/ alumni/loan communily. Unless you want to spend most of your day at your desk dealing with the minutia of expense reports, database entry, or outbound phone calls to clients and partners, I highly recommend you consider hiring a *Grinder*.

Let's take a moment lo revisit this role I first introduced in Section 3, The *Grinder* is the person who organizes the day-to-day business tasks, such as database management, outgoing lead generating phone calls, creating and printing flyers, pulling seminar and class packages together, tending to the *Finder's* schedule, event planning, expense reports and budgets, and more, This can either be one role or two, When your practice is large enough this will be the latter, The two roles are Database Manager and Marketing Director.

The *Grinder* role is so important. It is the coal that keeps our engine moving for ward. Without a well-defined database, as the *Finder* or *JV/inder,* you will have no clarity in the tasks, phone calls, status of loans, etc. from which to work from, If you forget to enter a new prospect or don't have pertinent information at your fin gertips-such as personal data, business goals, notes,loan features, or birthdays entered accurately-how could you possibly be able to follow up in a consistent and concise manner?

In mypractice I have the *Grinder* role broken into two different people, sometimes withthe same title and at other times the duties have been performed by separate individuals. Let me share my thoughts on this so you can be crystal clear when deciding how you would like to create job descriptions.

First,we have the Database Manager. This is the role withthe most administrative duties, This person does not have to be licensed as they will spend their days completing database entry for clients, partners, and transactions, For example, when you hold a seminar and return with 40 lo 50 business cards,your *Grinder* can enter all of the information into your CRM, prepare and send thank-you notes on your behalf, and initiate the drip campaign for the 70 days of communication. Then weekly, monthly, and quarterly they print reports for the *Finder* or *Minder* to utilize when making lead generating phone calls. The *Grinder* also schedules meeting spaces for events, prepares and sends monthly mailers, performs special projects, and completes expense reports.

Additionally, this *Grinder* is your retention manager as well. Every successful loan officer focuses on the business coming in, current business, *and* retaining the clients already gained or closed. If the information in your database isn't complete and accurate, you'll lose so many opportunities. The Database Manager role is critical in keeping the *Finder,* you, and the *Minder* focused on each of their spe cific roles so that nothing slips through the cracks.

Some *Grinders* can be licensed and in tandem with the Database Manager role. They can also conduct your outgoing phone calls to your active, passive, and credit prospects to nurture them until they are converted to live deals. They can contact your database to "check in" or to schedule annual reviews or call to wish people happy birthday.

The other *Grinder* role is that of Marketing Director. Again, this role can either be two separate positions or one single position, based on the volume of leads, loans, or activities that you as the *Finder* generate.

There are so many ideas available today to market your business. Of course, as the *Finder* you need to focus on relationship building as much as keeping in touch and staying top of mind with past clients.

While the Database Manager ensures that all contact information is complete and accurate, the Marketing Director (MD) is th e person who e ngag es with your database on numerous levels.

This individual is your liaison for marketing. The *Grinder* can organiz e a First-Time Home Buyer Seminar, a Meet & Greet My Team eve nt, or a Client Appreciation Event so prospects can see what it would be like to be in your community data base.

For your current and active clients, the MD will send milestone gifts and assist the *Finder* with recording video thank-you's and updates. Because this person is typi cally more outgoing than the Database Manager, they can also schedule meetings with new partners for the *Finder.*

Additionally, the MD can implement the drip campaign for the 70 days of com munication by sending predetermined emails, pho ne calls, marke ting items, and preparing pop -by items for the *Finder*. They can also make phone calls to obtain RSVPs for events and do social media postings.

Anything that will assist in generating new business, keeping active clients happy, and retaining referral partners and closed clients-without the need for a license is exactly the role this *Grinder* plays.

Having a *Grinder* to complete small, seemingly insignificant but extremely impor tant tasks will positively guarantee your ability to grow.

Jen's Jots

♦ Ensure you have a great CRM so that your entire team can utilize the func tions in their designated roles.

♦ Hire a Database Manager first. This is the most tedious of the *Grinder* tasks. You can continue to do the marketing tasks until you are too busy.

♦ Consider outsourcing marketing until your team grows to a level that you can hire a full-time Marketing Director.

✳ There's Gold in Those Names

> **The Big Idea:** Consistently grow, maintain, and use your contact community database to build long-term success,
>
> "He who sows sparingly will also reap sparingly, and he who sows bountifully will also reap bountifully."
>
> - 2 Corinthians 9:6

A lot of the ideas I've discussed in this book about how to grow your practice all have the same prerequisite: you should have a contact community to make them work. Particularly if you want to build long-term success, a contact community has no substitute.

You should view your contact community-your database of clients, prospects, real estate agents, referral partners of all kinds, service providers, really anyone who can influence your practice-as the heart of your business. It is, and will be, what pumps life into your practice. In fact, I'll bet that upwards of two-thirds of this year's business is sitting right there in your database. Why not take maximum
advantage of this resource?

A living, breathing contact community gives you so many paths to generating business that it's difficult to overstate its importance. You can leverage your con tact community to stay top of mind with clients so you can get into their "buying window." It is absolutely indispensable for tracking and following up on interac tions withyour referral partners.

If you act on the many ideas in this book on growing your contact community, you cannot help but succeed in this industry for many, many years to come.

Organization is Key

The first step in being able to use your community to grow your practice is getting your contact community in order. I often find when coaching loan officers across the country that their databases are fragmented and disorganized among several systems. Or even worse-in a notebook or on index cards, maybe even scraps of paper in an overstuffed file folder. Thisis *simply a somewhat unorganized collection of names, not a usable, orderly community.*

It's time to get all your prospects, clients, real estate agents, referral partners, and the like into one useful, usable database! It will make your life better and your business much more efficient.

Your contact community is the foundation of your mortgage practice and will cer tainly be the key to longevity and lasting success in the business. It deserves requisite attention and dedication-lots of love, care,and feeding!

If you don't use one now, at some point you must have a robust CRM-a customer relationship management or client relationship management system. What exactly is a CRM? A formal definition would be something like "a system used to manage and analyze customer interaction and data." It is more than just a database. The goal of using a CRM is to improve your relationships with clients, to help retain clients, and increase sales. A CRM will help you develop and track detailed infor mation on clients and partners-such as birthdays and anniversaries-so you can develop a more personal relationship.

A CRM can be used to automate many, many tasks in a mortgage practice, such as marketing. This is where the efficiency advantages of a CRM really come into play.

Yes,CRMs can be pricey,but for a mortgage practice a high-quality system can be obtained by paying a monthly per-user license fee. It is a worthwhile investment. Nothing will pay higher dividends over the long term.

So ditch the Excel-based database and automate your piles of paper. Take full advantage of the power of a CRM program. Once you discover the power and features of today's CRMs, your imagination will runwild on how you can use it.

A CRM's power will go to waste if you don't get organized. If your contact commu nity records are in disarray, gather and/or print all your contacts from your various sources. Categorize them according to:

♦   Those you want to expand your association with,

♦   Those you want to limit your association with,

♦   And those you want to disassociate with altogether.

You will also want to further categorize contacts according to what role they have in your practice. From there, build and refine your CRM contact community to tailor it to your practice and your way of doing business.

Then you'll want to be organized daily to grow and maintain your CRM; this is why it's soimportant to have a separate *Grinder* doing this job. If it'sjust you,well,you really will have to slot some time blocks for this activity. Your community will be ever-growing, changing,and evolving. But your CRM will notpayitsbig dividends if you ignore maintenance and updating for weeks or months at a time!Investigate your options. Some systems have features that enable importing data from other software or systems. This feature could make maintenance less of a chore for you.

Gold Standard

Your CRM is like a solid block of gold. Your other marketing and outreach activi ties will help you find small flakes and nuggets, but your living, breathing contact community will lead you straight to the mother lode.

Your contact CRM enables you to keep in touch with clients as frequently as pos sible. You can be in front of clients and referral partners to stay top of mind and to be able to identify and act on opportunities. There are a multitude of reasons to call people; a well-maintained and updated contact community enables you to build a record of a client's history or a partner's interests and then use that information to stay close to them.

It is quite likely that if you are diligent about building and maintaining your data base, you will grow it over the years to 1,000, 2,000, or more contacts. But even if you start out with just 50 or 100 contacts in your community, by making use of it to reach out regularly to clients and partners, you will see immediate results in your practice.

Jen's Jots

♦ Invest in a customer relationship management system to be able to lever age your contact community for business growth. Your investment willpay off manytimes over.

♦ Follow a system and regular schedule for adding to and maintaining your contact community to keep it as useful as possible.

✳ Tools of the Trade

> **The Big Idea:** Use automated tools and utilities to make your operations as efficient as possible and your client service extraordinary.
>
> "The only place where success comes before work is in the dictionary."
>
> - Vidal Sassoon

The past several years have ushered in a new era of powerful tools, utilities, and applications that enable you to do things in your loan process that save you a lot of time and help push your client service to new heights. Applications for smart phones and tablets have added another dimension to how you can serve clients.

Of course, you might not actually get more efficient in your processes if you just gather a bunch of "gee-whiz" apps. No, first you need to determine what process you want to follow and what makes sense for you and your practice. You can find many references online about "the perfect loan process;" but what it really means is the perfect process for *your practice* and how you operate.

Before you can apply any tool or app, you first must determine how it fits into *and helps* the process you use. After all, if it doesn't make your process better, faster, more efficient, easier to accomplish, etc., what's the point?

Understand that when you put together your perfect loan process or any process, you need to understand the scope of what is available to you. This is from a financial perspective, in terms of the skill sets you and your team have, and how it fits into what you want to undertake.

I think it's really important that you craft your own perfect loan process and not try to wedge a canned process into your operations. Make sure when you're setting up your perfect loan process that you have the resources to fulfill the things that you're putting in the process. Even in my own process, there are a few items I'd like to implement but haven't yet because I haven't found the right resource.

How to get started you ask? First, lay out what you want to accomplish and how you want to provide impeccable seNice to others. Define exactly and precisely what happens and how you want to manage and/or react-each step, action or task-from lead-to-years after closing a loan, creating the best framework that you possibly can. Understand that you may not be able to implement all actions imme diately. Just dream. Put together what you think you want to have in your process, and if you're not able to put it all into practice right away, that's fine. When you do find the right utility or app, and have the financial wherewithal to acquire and use that tool, then consider incorporating it into your process at that time.

Some Tools and Utilities That I Use in My Process

I want to share with you some of the resources that I use as part of my perfect loan process. These tools and utilities help me accomplish so much in such a short period of time. Three of my most powerful tools are holding the Certified Mortgage Planning Specialist designation, Mortgage Coach Edge to demonstrate to my clients the true cost of a mortgage over a specified time, and MBS Highway for monitoring mortgage backed security markets.

My number one tool is that of me holding the designation of an Advanced Certified Mortgage Planning Specialist (Advanced-CMPS). This is an enormous differentiator in my practice, as it takes me from being a commodity to being an expert. The ability to manipulate lending rules and guidelines in a positive man ner to represent the needs of my clients through mortgage planning strategies sets me apart from hundreds of thousands of traditional loan officers. Having the ability to provide continuing education to Financial Advisors has been priceless in expanding my referral partner community and thereby my closed loan volume. Gibran Nicholas is one of the most intelligent, thoughtful, and giving men I've ever known. I thank him for his expertise and guidance to ensure the quality of education in our industry.

My second favorite tool is Mortgage Coach Edge. This online and mobile software is invaluable for my practice. I can stream live with my clients, record audio or video summaries of mortgage financing options in a manner no Excel spreadsheet or Loan Operating System could ever perform. Thank you to Dave Savage for his endless quest for advancement of our loan officer community.

Third in my arsenal is MBS Highway. It is critical for any loan officer to know exactly what is affecting daily global, financial, and mortgage markets. The adage of simply answering interest rates questions from clients on where we think rates are heading of "well, if I had a crystal ball about rates, I'd be retired and on a beach somewhere" simply won 't work in our highly competitive market. Barry Habib shares daily morning market updates that can easily be learned and under stood by any loan officer or team member. The tools provided are so valuable to my everyday activities.

I also use Bomb Bomb, which is a video recording app. I can email a video record ing to a client to say hello, update them on market conditions, talk about annual reviews, and on and on. The options are endless. The email embeds my logo and other branding and marketing features to add value with a personal touch.

In addition to being a CMPS, I am also a Certified Divorce Lending Professional (COLP). This designation has opened so many doors with financial services experts such as financial planners and divorce and estate planning attorneys that I may have not been able to reach otherwise.

Another very handy tool I use is Mortgage Mapp, which is an app I use daily that allows partners and clients to easily and efficiently refer me. Rather than hand ing out a business card, which most likely will get thrown away within days, my app sits right on the user's mobile device. It's a subliminal reminder of me and my services. Clients can request meetings with me, inquire about prequalifying, calculate affordability for themselves, and even stay informed on interest rate market conditions.

MileIQ is fantastic for logging mileage. This app has been approved by the IRS, so there is no need to manually record odometer readings. You can also categorize any trip into personal or business, with subcategories for specific activities, which really keeps record-keeping organized.

Calendly enables clients to schedule appointments with me so we don't waste time or get frustrated with endless back-and-forth calls and emails trying to sched ule an appointment. The app also connects to Outlook. You can use Calendly on your desktop, laptop, and mobile device. I can't tell you how much time this has saved me!

An app I suggest to my clients is called Moving Day. As part of my process, I send a link to the app so they can begin working on their moving and packing plan.

I also utilize Doodle for scheduling appointments and conference calls with sev eral different people. I organize, and participate in, frequent panels so when I'm trying to coordinate the members of a panel, this is a great tool to use. Individuals can select all of the suggested times and dates that work for them, making it easy to reach digital consensus on a meeting time. Again, it saves an enormous amount of time and effort compared to the back and forth with multiple emails.

Another very handy tool is EverNote, which I use to record my intake notes for referrals. I can track the referrals I receive, and categorize them according to whether they're looking, or on hold, or if they become a live deal.

Most of you have heard of Fiverr, which I use to find people to perform some *Grinding* tasks, such as designing flyers, or producing spreadsheets, or editing my recordings for my podcasts. I use Fiverr for anything and everything. If you don't want, or don't know how to make a flyer or presentation, or you want someone to do some simple *Grinding* work for you to save your time, it's a good place to get the task done in less than 24 hours. It's also a good source to find a virtual administrative assistant or a team member.

I use MGIC's app to quickly determine PMI for a client. I think Radian and UGIC might have similar tools. I like MGIC's, but whatever one works for you, it's a good thing to have at your fingertips.

When I go to a networking event or teach a business class and I collect every one's business card, I use CamCard to take a photo of the card, which is instantly imported into Outlook. Just like that I have contact information for everybody, saving me even more precious time. You will need to check the accuracy to make sure it's picking up the details correctly, because some business cards contain information that cannot be read.

I use DropBox to share documents. It's great because I can have it on my cell phone as well as on my computer, allowing me to review documents quickly. If I'm on my boat and I need to do a pre-approval letter, I can do it right from my cell phone, save it to DropBox, and send the link to the real estate agent.

A utility that I recently added and am in love with is called PreApp1003. It's an online and mobile tool for your clients to securely and quickly complete their loan application. You can send a link to clients to fill out a quick application or ask them to text a word you create to a text number you are assigned. You can then import the information into your LOS with ease. You may have similar capability through your company. I don't, so for me this is a game changer in the ability to obtain data faster, with a great client experience as well.

Tools and utilities can make operations, transactions, and prospecting highly auto mated and therefore very efficient. They are great time savers and many of them contribute tremendously to making your team more efficient.

Of course, the tools I've talked about here are just the tip of the iceberg when considering the application of automation to your practice. When you look for a tool or utility to use within your process and practice, be sure to ask colleagues for recommendations.

Jen's Jot's

♦ Before you try to apply any new tool or utility to your operations, deter mine if it truly fits into what you want to accomplish.

♦ Don't build your perfect loan process around whatever tools and utilities you come across. First decide what you want your process to be and then search for the ideal tools.

For More Information

For more information on the utilities and tools mentioned in this chapter, visit these sites:

NOTE: Deleted items are not mentioned in the text.

- Bomb Bomb - http://bombbomb.com
- Calendly - https://calendly.com
- CamCard - https://www.camcard.com
- Certified Divorce Lending Professional - http://www. divorcelendingassociation.com
- Certified Mortgage Planning Specialist - https://www. cmpsinstitute.org
- Doodle - http://doodle.com
- DropBox - http://www.dropbox.com
- EverNote - https://evernote.com
- Fiverr - https://www.fiverr.com
- MBS Highway - https://www.mbshighway.com
- MGIC - https://www.mgic.com/mobileapp
- MileIQ - https://www.mileiq.com
- Mortgage Coach - https://mortgagecoach.com
- Mortgage Mapp - http://www.mortgagemapp.com
- Moving Day by Mighty Ants - Look in the Apple Store
- PreApp 1003 - https://preapp1003.com
- Radian - http://www.radian.biz
- UGIC - https://www.ugcorp.com

✳ Who's Managing Your Mortgage?

> **The Big Idea:** You can grow the size of your database (and your business!) by leaps and bounds with ones imple question: Who's Managing Your Mortgage?
>
> *"Don't ever allow yourself to get bored with your client's most expensive purchase-it isn't fair to your client"*
>
> *- Jen DuPlessis*

It's a simple question, really, but one a lot of people don't understand. It is also one of *THE* most powerful ways to expand the size of your contact database and thus add to your business.

The question is: 'Who's managing your mortgage?" This simple question can change the course of your business because it continually hands you clients for long-term growth.

What Is It, Really?

A typical client will answer with the name of the loan seNicing company. Believe me I've asked this question thousands of times. We all know that the servicing company is NOT interested in managing the mortgage, but merely collecting pay ments.

Here's an example of why this is so important. If you asked that same client,"Who manages your assets?" they would answer with "Oh,that would be Bob Money. He's been managing our retirement funds for years." They don't even know who Bob works for, they just know HIM.

Good 01' Bob! Listen, you want to be Bob, but in the mortgage space! Only you will be managing a client's debt rather than their assets. This is exactly what a Certified Mortgage Planning Specialist does.

As a professional mortgage loan officer, you should focus on the entrance strat egy in obtaining a mortgage loan as well as the exit strategy (this is why we ask the question about how long the client thinks they will stay in the home, or have the loan). What is often overlooked is the period of time that your client is holding their mortgage loan.

Sure, you send mailers and make occasional phone calls (well, at least you did prior to reading this book, right?), but what about all of the life events that happen during the course of homeownership and the impact those could have on your client's ability to maintain a perpetual pre-approval should they need to mover earlier than expected or want to move as planned?

Managing a client's mortgage is about being in touch with them regularly between the time they close on their loan until the time they pay off their loan. During this time you can differentiate yourself from other loan officers by conducting the annual review, as I've talked about previously, but also through timely touches to update the homeowner on mortgage market conditions, Federal Reserve comments and adjustments, home improvement tips that assist with strong returns on value, identity theft consultations (pulling credit and reviewing the findings with the client to safeguard any surprises for future loans), early payoff strategies, ARM to Fixed consultations and insurances, elimination of Private Mortgage Insurance, initiating an auto-lock opportunity so that when rates drop you won't have to make hundreds of calls or miss out altogether because you didn't have your CRM complete and accurate, and asking for referrals of course.

Keep yourself top of mind with literally hundreds or thousands (as you keep building your database over the years!) of clients. You can grow your future loan database by managing their mortgage, even if you didn't originate the loan. Why not "adopt" their mortgage? They were most likely "orphaned" by their last lender as soon as the ink was dry on the closing papers. You can gain tremendous trust with these clients by revisiting their entrance, holding, and exit strategy so that they stay on track with their goals. Oh, wait, they didn't have a strategy or goals because their original lender didn't bother to inquire? Get my point?!

This has been one of my biggest secrets for years. I began this because had to manage clients' loans to protect their interests. The only product I had was a negatively amortizing loan (before it was widespread and dealt to loan officers who had no business selling). I discovered the importance and genuine need to educate and communicate with my alumni clients because most of them would forget how their loan worked. I grew closer to them and became a valued advisor and expert in the process.

Look, we all know it's a numbers game. The more people you have in our database, the more business you do. The key lies in what and how you keep yourself engaged.

Your *Grinder,* or you, if you are managing this role currently, can contact each of the clients in your CRM a minimum of four to five times a year. I learned this great tip from Carl White of Mortgage Marketing Animals when I attended one of his three-day high-impact workshops in Tampa, Florida.

First, there are 52 weeks in a year, there are 26 letters in the alphabet. So, the first week of January call everyone, and I mean everyone (clients, prospects, partners, vendors), in your database whose last name begins with A. The second week call the Bs, third week the Cs, and so on. When the first of July rolls around you will have contacted everyone in your database. You can also double up and call the As and Bs the first week, Cs and Ds the second week, and so on, and the result will be that you will touch each contact four times in a year. You can print or refresh your reports quarterly so that any new clients can be included in the rotation sooner rather than later.

Let's assume you utilize the one-alphabet-letter-a-week campaign. That would result in a minimum of two touches per year. Next, call each client whose mort gage is being managed on the anniversary date of them purchasing their home or closing on their refinance. That's now a total of three touches. Lastly, call each contact either on Memorial Day or Veterans Day if they are a U.S. veteran, or on Thanksgiving or at the New Year to say "Thank you for being such a great client and important part of my practice. I simply couldn't do it without your trust, sup port, and continued referrals." By my count that is now four to five touches in a year.

Go one step further and call each contact on their birthday. Again, let me remind you that your *Grinder* can make these calls for you as long as they are licensed because you want to anticipate that the call will generate questions about loans and rates or result in new referrals.

There are special occasions such as birthdays, wedding anniversaries, births, engagements, and yes, even sympathy events. As long as you are actively engag ing with your contacts you will be aware of any life changes or events.

You can send RateWatch Reports, updated Mortgage Coach Edge reports after conducting an annual review, CMPS newsletters, email newsletters, and so on. An opportunity for reaching out is created whenever there is a shift in the market.

There are so many reasons for you to call, email, text, IM, or send a video. The options are limitless. Just be confident and true to yourself by only engaging in marketing that resonates with you.

As a reminder, all of these ideas cannot be implemented overnight and should only be implemented based on your budget, resources, utilitie s, and most impor tantly your ability to block the time to get the tasks done! (Sounds like you might need a Marketing Director *Grinder.*)

Perfect Question for Referral Partners

You certainly want to manage the mortgage of the clients who secured loans through you or another lender who you were later referred.

I'd like to offer a little bonus to you. Would that be okay with you?

If you want to expand your database two-fold, leverage the reach of your referral partners. This is what I have done for years. Referral partners, particularly those in financial and legal services, can be a goldmine in this area.

Simply help your referral partners refer business to you by encouraging them, partnering with them, and training them on how to ask their clients (I imagine each has a database of at least 250 contacts): "Who's Managing Your Mortgage?"

Their client answers the question and that provides your referral partner with an opening to say, "Well, you know, I have a fantastic mortgage planner on my team. She manages mortgages for several of my clients. This is a complimentary service to you as a client of mine. May I introduce you to her?" The rest is up to you.

Conduct an initial annual review with them and then fold them right into your data base management process. They will either refinance, buy another home, or refer their friends and colleagues at some point during your management of their loan.

Don't forget to offer the same partnership opportunity to your realtor partners.

Each of your partners will need continuing education and reinforcement, so be sure to mention your mortgage management program frequently.

Jen's Jots

♦ Educate financial sector referral partners and realtors to ask their clients, "Who's Managing Your Mortgage?"

♦ Once these clients are in your database, communicate with them on a regular basis to keep you top of mind and put yourself in a position for their future business.

✳ Grinder Tasks/Roles/Activities

> **The Big Idea:** Sample list of Grinder activities to get you started
>
> "If you care at all, you'll get some results,
> If you care enough, you'll get incredible results."
>
> -Jim Rohn

Database Manager

- Database content quality.
- Database entry all contacts.
- Finder Assistant.
- Manage all reports for Minder and Finder for prospecting, nurturing, active clients, retention, and partners.
- Prepare expense reports.
- Order supplies.
- Manage RateWatch and Managed Mortgage Reports and mailers.
- Write thank-you notes.
- Special projects.
- Assist Marketing Director Grinder with event preparation.
- Schedule meeting locations.
- Prepare monthly income and expense report.
- Assist Finder for meeting preparation/agenda.
- Daily huddle.

Marketing Director

- liaison for marketing department.
- Manage details of all events/classes.

- Monthly newsletter email and mailing.
- Social Media-posts, biogs, likes, comments, invites, connections, and notifications for Finder.
- Create presentations/flyers.
- Schedule meetings with partners.
- Special projects.
- Prepare pop-by items for Finder.
- Schedule delivery of Milestone gifts.
- Manage 70-day campaign emails, phone calls, marketing material.
- Video marketing for Finder.
- Write thank-you notes.
- Obtain promotional items.
- Manage yearly marketing calendar.

SECTION 7.

WHAT HAPPENS NEXT?

✳ Be a Life Learner

The Big Idea: The KEY to continual advancement in this industry and growing your practice is to embrace constant learning.

"Formal education will make you a living.
Self-education will make you a fortune."

-Jim Rohn

By no means is our industry static. Far from it! The way things change so con stantly it's getting harder and harder to be on the cutting edge.

Compliance keeps changing, guidelines keep changing, the way people find us has really changed, the way people get loans has changed tremendously.

You have to constantly stay ahead of the cuNe, or you'll fall farther and farther behind. The way to stay ahead is to embrace being a lifelong learner.

Standing Still · Going Backward

In our industry today, if you're not moving forward, you're actually moving back ward. You're not even standing still, you're moving backward because things change so much and so constantly.

Think about when you first got into the business and you didn't know anything. You had to dedicate yourself to learning and being a student of the industry. You didn't know what loan products were,you had to study underwriting guidelines and perhaps attempt to be a salesperson. You needed to talk to and work with your loan processor and your underwriter to understand the process. You had to learn about the market and how rates tick,you had to learn loan-level pricing,and you had to figure out how to price a loan. You determined how to qualify some body, what income you could use, and whatyou couldn't use.

There were a thousand and one things you had to learn. You had to educate yourself so you could be a knowledgeable loan originator.

All of that learning got you to this point. Now,though,you may be challenged by how the industry has changed andyou mayfeel stumped. At one time you feltyou had the necessary knowledge, but don't feel that way anymore.

Challenge Questions

If you'ro fooling liko you'ro loeing ground in the knowledge game, it's time to challenge yourself!

So I have some questions for you. The answers will reveal to you whether you are challenging yourself to move forward or if you're falling behind.

- Are you any different today after the huge changes to our market than you were prior to Dodd-Frank and the TRID disclosure rule? Do you truly know how TRID works and what the disclosure timeline requirements are? Have you taken additional steps to improve since the advent of these immense changes?

- Have you read a self-improvement or business book in the last six months? And if you have, do you remember the name of it? Do you remember what it was about? Did you try to apply at least one new idea that you learned in the book?

- Do you read any mortgage-specific magazines that come to your office or home? Do you read them front-to-back or do you just look at some statis tics? Do you dig in and read so that you can learn something new? Do you even subscribe to industry magazines?

- + In the last six months, have you looked at and mastered a new product that you could sell? Even better, have you looked at, end-to-end, guide lines from one of your investors, if you're a correspondent or broker, or your own company's guidelines?

- + Do you regularly attend seminars, conferences, webinars, listen to pod casts such as Mortgage Lending Mastery (shameless self-promotion of my podcast), or watch YouTube videos on topics in, or related to, your industry?

- Do you subscribe to any newsletters about sales? Or about positive think ing? Or about motivation? If you haven't, subscribe to those, then read or listen to them every single day.

- Do you have a business coach? To move forward, you need an account ability partner, which a coach can fulfill.

- Are you an active member of an industry board or committee such as the Mortgage Banker's Association, Mortgage Broker's Association, National Association of Professional Mortgage Women, or others?

- Here's another one. Have you attended a seminar held in our industry by one of our associations in the last six months? Are you even a member or an affiliate member of an association?

Are you a HAS or a HAS BEEN? You know it's one thing to move the needle for ward on your business on a daily basis, and that's working irr your business. This is working on your business...and on yourself.

One Last Question

What are you doing to continually develop your talents and skills, to strengthen your commitment to your career so you can get smarter and better in the mort gage industry?

Jen's Jots

♦ The industry keeps getting more complex and challenging. The only way to stay ahead is to keep learning.

♦ Embrace kaizen, the process of continuous improvement. If you're not improving every day, you're losing ground.

♦ Read at least 10 pages of a business, self-improvement, or real estate related book every day. Make time to read! Ten pages a day adds up to 3,650 pages a year, anywhere from 15 to 20 books. That's a ton of knowl edge right there!

♦ Listen to podcasts, either mine or others, to expand your growth and wealth of knowledge. Listen during "downtime," when you're waiting in line or driving to the office or ho me. I'll bet youcould get in one to two hours of learning every week.

♦ Cross-pollinate your knowledge. Learn abou t taxes and real estate and finance so you have a comprehensive view of how mortgage lending fits in.

♦ Learn about tax implications with a CPA. Talk to estate p lanners to learn more about estate planning. These topics have a bearing on mortgage lending.

♦ Develop and/or improve your perso nal and sa le s skills .

Th e bottom line is that when you challenge yourself, you can educate and better inform and guide your clients. Whe n an "intern " is asked a question such as "Can you give me an idea of where the rates going?" an intern will say someth ing like, "O h, if I knew that, if I had a crystal ball, I'd be lounging on a beach somewhere!" When a "Ph.D." is asked that same question, the Ph.D. off ers a sophistic ated answer because the Ph.D. has his or her head wrapped around mortgage-backed securities, how they work , and what's happening in the economy. A Ph.D. under stands what the federal funds rat e is and how it impacts short-term rates, not long-term rates. Are you an intern or Ph.D.?

✳ Designations Demonstrate Your Expertise

> **The Big Idea:** Separate yourself from the competition by earning a professional designation.
>
> *"If you have integrity, nothing else matters; if you don't have integrity, nothing else matters."*
>
> *- Harvey MacKay*

Your credibility as a professional is going to be vitally important as we move into the future. We've had tremendous turmoil in the industry the past ten years, and the challenges and competition that face us in the future will keep growing, You will need to elevate your professionalism and be able to demonstrate your exper tise in order to compete effectively, You particularly must do everything you can to rise from being a commodity to a preferred product provider.

Pressure for demonstrating your expertise is coming from many directions. People these days are extremely conscious about reviewing capabilities and experience online to find someone who can clearly demonstrate they are a legitimate, edu cated, credentialed, professional mortgage expert. Those expectations are certain to affect how all of us will be evaluated in the future.

Pressure is also coming from within our industry, specifically to be licensed and recognized as true professionals.

If you don't have any professionally-recognized acronym after your name, and your card simply says you're a loan offer, senior loan officer, or mortgage consul tant, I think it's vitally important that you get further education and training and obtain one or more professional designations,

Why do I think this is so important to your future?

First, it shows your commitment to being a **professional,** It shows that you're willing to dedicate your time, energy, and focus to ensure that you're an expert. It shows you're knowledgeable and that you're at the forefront of knowing what is happening in our industry, You are familiar with the techniques for dealing with retirement and saving and taxes. And you know about alternatives, and even some of the older options in the market. I can't stress enough how important your level of professionalism goes above and beyond the mainstream basics of the industry.

For those of you who have been in the industry a long time, you've seen people jump into our industry,make a lot of money,create havoc,and then leave because they couldn't make it over the long term. They've leftuswith having to pick up the pieces from what they destroyed, quitefrankly.

We have to regularly discuss and demonstrate how lenders are professional advi sors rather than have everyone think of us as just run-of-the-mill service providers.

Your commitmentto obtaining a professional designation also bolsters your **integrity.** When you have a designation, it demonstrates thatyou care. You care about
your industry, you care aboutyour image and your brand not just for yourself but your industry as a whole. That goes a long way to building trust. People love to work withpeople theytrust.

A designation also shows you are **ethical.** This is how you make a living, this is important to you, and you don't want anything to destroy that. You're cognizant of any fraudulent activities, and you're aware of any peripheral activities by other parties around you. Having strong ethics is very important.

The last aspect to your professional designation is that it demonstrates your com mitment to your **fiduciary responsibility.** You are responsible for guiding people properly through a complex process-you're supposed to be the expert! The cli ent is a lay person, and you have the responsibility to direct them in the optimum way to meet their goals and needs, not to merely satisfy your income and produc tion goals.

Industry Designations

I want to talk about some of these designations.

The first one, and this is important to me because it is one of the designations that I have and that I've had for a long time, is the Certified Mortgage Planning Specialist, otherwise known as CMPS. This is a 15-hour self-study course, but you can also take a class to get the certification.

The CMPS studycovers these principal areas:
♦ Mortgage and real estate taxation.
♦ Housing, financial, and mortgage markets.
♦ Cash flow planning for homeowners and buyers.
♦ Cash flow planning for real estate investors.
♦ Ethics and compliance.

The CMPS designation places you in unique company. There are fewer than 1,000 of us in the country. Think about this: there are about 600,000 loan officers right now in the country, and about 140,000 or 150,000 are licensed loan officers, whereas the balance of the 600,000 are loan officers who work at banks and are not required to go through the license testing but do have a registered license. With approximately 1,000 Certified Mortgage Planning Specialists, you wonder how everyone else is representing their clients?

With this designation, you could place yourself head-and-shoulders above your competition. You'll have a greater understanding of cash flow, tax benefits, wealth building, as well as entrance, maintenance, and exit strategies for a loan that are aligned with financial, estate, and retirement planning. You'll have greater confi dence and expertise to advise clients on the biggest purchase they'll ever make.

The second designation that I'd like to talk about and one I've recently obtained is the CDLP, Certified Divorce Lending Professional. This is an eight-hour self study course plus test. The Certified Divorce Lending Professional is someone who knows much more about crucial aspects of such areas as dividing marital property and pairing that with mortgage lending. This knowledge is vital to help one of the divorcing spouses to, for example, continue to remain in their home and not uproot their children.

The study for the CDLP is eye-opening; it is a great designation, and the knowl edge you get from studying for the CDLP enables you to provide some very valu able advice.

Another reason I elected to get both the CDLP and the CMPS designations is that each of them allows me to teach continuing education credits, which establishes me as a subject matter expert in the eyes of the audience I'm teaching.

In the case of the CMPS designation, I can provide continuing education cred its to new financial advisors up to Certified Financial Planners. This is extremely important for me because I wanted to have multiple income streams and referral sources.

A variety of designations are available through the Institute of Mortgage Lending of the National Association of Professional Mortgage Women. Now, these certifi cations are not just for women, men are welcome to take them. In fact, a few years ago the President of NAPMW was a man. The IML / NAPMW certifications are:

♦ Graduate of Mortgage Lending

♦ Master of Mortgage Lending (MML)

- ◆ Certified Mortgage Instructor (CMI)
- ◆ Certified in Mortgage Ethics (CME)

You can get well-known designations through the Mortgage Bankers Association the number one designation offered is Certified Mortgage Banker or CMB. That's a very well-respected designation. Your tenure in the business can give you a head start on obtaining that designation. With a long tenure in the business, you can pass through many layers of education and reduce the amount of time you would have to spend in taking the testing and getting that designation.

The Certified Mortgage Banker designation is made up of several levels, namely the *Residential CMB, Commercial CMB, Executive CMB, and Master CMB. Another designation available through the MBA is the* Accredited Mortgage Professional (AMP),

The prestige of having a designation or two can get diluted if you have too many, so do some research and find something that works for you, something that really resonates with you. Attaining a designation will make you feel, demonstrate, and know that you have taken the time to continue your education to elevate yourself to a professional level in an increasingly competitive marketplace.

Jen's Jots

- ◆ Obtaining one or more industry designations demonstrates your commit ment to professionalism, integrity, ethics, and fiduciary responsibility for your clients.
- ◆ Studying for a designation gives you the knowledge that will help you bet ter serve and advise your clients.

1st and 10s a Glance

Certified Mortgage Planning Specialist (CMPS)-See the CMPS Institute at: www.cmpsinstitute.org

Certified Divorce Lending Professional (CDLP)-See the Divorce Lending & Real Estate Association at: www.divorcelendingassociation.com/cdlp.html

For the following certifications, see the Institute of Mortgage Lending of the National Association of Professional Mortgage Women at: www.napmw.org/?educationlML

- ◆ Graduate of Mortgage Lending
- ◆ Master of Mortgage Lending (MML)
- ◆ Certified Mortgage Instructor (CMI)
- ◆ Certified in Mortgage Ethics (CME)

For the Certified Mortgage Banker designation, see the Mortgage Bankers Association at www.mba.org

For the Accredited Mortgage Professional (AMP), designed for those in mortgage industry management, see the Mortgage Bankers Association at www.mba.org

✳ Stepping Stone to a Secure Future

> **The Big Idea:**Use your mortgage lending career as astepping stone to a secure financial future by investing in real property.
>
> "We all need lots of powerful long-range goals...to help usget past the short-term obstacles"
>
> -JimRohn

Do you see mortgage lending as a life-long career? I truly hope so. I hope you can build a career that has staying power for 25, 30, or more years.

While I believe a long-term career in this industry will give you financial success, what I wish for you is long-term financial *independence.* And for that you need to think outside of day-to-day lending and investigate long-term investments.

What do I mean by financial independence? Well, one way to look at it is this: If you can walk away from your mortgage practice today, and still have enough income coming in to live your current lifestyle,you're financially independent.

Your mortgage practice can be a stepping stone to investments that deliver pas sive income streams to you now and for the long-term. We don't have pension plans or retirement income in this industry, so it's up to us to create a secure future for ourselves. Rather than just focus on transactions month after month, wondering where your next paycheck is going to come from,I believe you can use the money you're earning today to create wealth for your future.

Practice What YouPreach

As you know, I do a lot of teaching, especially for real estate agents. I'm continu ally amazed at how many agents own just one house. They don't own 2, or 5, or 10, or more properties,they own one house. It's amazing to me that someone who is selling real estate can tell someone thatthis is a fantastic time to buy or sell,and yet they're not buying the product. To me, that's preposterous! It's just like some one selling Mary Kay cosmetics and saying, well, these are fantastic cosmetics. I don't use them, but you should buy them. Instead,I use Estee Lauder.

Think that sounds crazy? Guess what, it may be just as crazy on our part too, if you're not investing in real estate. I have found that many of us in mortgage lending don't have more than one property,either. Why don'tyou own more than one property? Do you practice what you preach?

Daily, as a lender,you tell clients that mortgage rates are great, it's a great time to buy,and so much wealth can be gained by owning real estate. Yet why aren't you buying more real estate? Don't you believe in the productyou are selling?

There is another part to this. I hear a lot of people talk about making a lot of money, but what are they doing with it? Is your money working for you, or are you working just to have money? I can't tell you howmany times I have been to conferences and business mixers with other mortgage people who brag about what they have or show off a $10,000 watch. Are you kidding me? That money, andthis is just my opinion, but that $10,000 could be the closing costs for a rental property. That money could be the down payment for a rental property that brings in income for years and years to come. And that's not even taking into consider ationthe appreciation of the property.

Your role is to be a strategic financial partner to your clients. And yet, with the knowledge and expertise you have,you maynot be doing as much as you should for yourself. Now, if I'm preaching to the choir,fantastic. Congratulations to you, because you've figured it out. But if you haven't, if you haven't bought that first rental property,it'stime to get on the ball.

Take action. Put a plan in place to sustainyour income when you eventually leave lending.

Additionally, it's crucial for you to, one, save money in your 401k, your Roth IRA, whatever your financial advisor recommends and you agree to. Then two, start investing and buying properties. We chase the deal all our lives. Wouldn't it be nice to go out to the mailbox and have income coming in when you're out of lend ing, or to supplement lending when you go through good and bad times? You know we all have rolling hills-there are times when our income is a little higher, times when it's a little lower. There's not a one of us that closes the exact same number of loans every single month. It's incredibly important to have supplemen tal passive income.

Jen's Jots

♦ Plan from the very beginning of your mortgage lending practice to develop passive streams of income that give you financial independence when you finish your career.

♦ Take your own advice and investin real property to build a secure financial future.

By ibran Nicholas

Jen's energy is contagious, and her passion for life and people is truly an inspira tion. That's a lot to say for someone who's been tossed and turned by life and career in the way that she has been! I think that's what makes her story so com pelling. We can all identify with her ups and downs, and yet we can also see ourselves emerging triumphant through it all.

That's why the lessons you've read in this book are so incredibly valuable. They are not theoretical. They are practical, and they've been tested in the real world. This book was not written by an academic in an ivory tower. It was written by a practitioner who's in the trenches every day. The ideas are not "big picture" and the words are not cliches. They are at once strategic, tactical, and filled with meaning.

For example, when Jen talks about teams and time management, I've actually seen her system humming along in full swing. When we were traveling the country together on a speaking tour not too long ago, she was out of her office for weeks at a time. Her business was running smoothly in her absence, and she wasn't con stantly on the phone putting out fires. When she was on the phone, it was doing what she does best: leading her team and giving her mortgage clients world-class advice. Jen's system allows her to focus on the truly important things, and that's what empowers her to make a difference.

We all have the same 1,440 minutes in a 24-hour day. The difference between experiencing excellence or mediocrity in our life is found in how we choose to invest those minutes. I assure you that every minute you spent invested in this book will result in a tremendous improvement in your life and business...IF you implement. My best suggestion for you now that you've read this book is to:

♦   Pick out one or two strategies and tactics that you believe you can imple ment right away.

♦   Go and actually DO those one or two things.

♦   Repeat steps 1-2 over and over again!

According to Duke University researchers, about 40% of the actions we take as human beings each day are not intentional or deliberate acts. They are habits. That's why it's so important to take Jen's tactics and plug-and-play them into your daily routine. Pick the ones that really speak to you. For example, if you feel like the urgent items in your life and business are enslaving you at the expense of the important, reread Section 3 of this book. If you feel like you're struggling for busi ness when you shouldn't be, go back to Section 2 of this book. In all cases, enjoy the read, because Jen's personality is super-fun!

One more thing: this is not a typical business book with business advice. Nor is it a self-help book for personal inspiration. It's a true story...an unfolding drama...a gripping thriller, starring YOU as the hero and main character. The ending is not yet written. That's YOUR part. The whole point of Jen's message is that you can have a successful business AND a successful family AND a fulfilling, happy, and meaningful life. This book contains the story of a remarkable woman, who beat remarkable odds, to live a remarkable life. That's YOUR story too...but only if you LAUNCH and take action.

Jen's hope, and mine as well, is that one day soon, we'll find ourselves sitting around a table with you drinking a fine Italian wine and toasting your remarkable journey! Until then, buckle your seatbelt (or snuggle up in bed) and have a very enjoyable and impactful reading experience!

I'm always interested in meeting with you to discuss how you can spark or re spark your practice! Whether you'd prefer a one-to-one coaching session, sales training, a company meeting, or a corporate consulting event, please feel free to contact me at Jen@kineticsparkconsulting.com or at kineticsparkconsulting.com

Be sure to also listen in to my podcast, "Mortgage Lending Mastery," on iTunes for additional insights and advice on how to take your mortgage practice to new heights!